SURVIVING THE WILDERNESS

On the Way to Your Destiny

Priscar Manei

ISBN: 978-0-9565780-5-1

Published by:

Manei Publications

Printed in the United States of America and the United Kingdom

FOREWORD

Priscar Manei is a true servant of God. She has faithfully served in our European branch of Ministry for the past several years. She has displayed the utmost loyalty and diligence in her service to us and to God. Her book will bless you in various ways, but mostly because it is revelation born out of true experience in her walk with Almighty God. We pray this book will reach and bless multitudes in many nations. Send us your testimonies and comments to: Ministry@ThomasManton.com. Visit us Online: www.ThomasManton.com.

Dr. Thomas Manton IV
CEO/Founder ~ Dominion International

I have known Priscar for many years; I saw her come to faith in Jesus as she answered God's call on her life. Since those early days in Nairobi, she has walked closely with God, seeking to do His will, persevering through difficult times and enduring hardship. She never complains, and she turns problems into prayers - truly a Godly woman! This book is a result of a life lived for our Lord. Eternal truths tried and tested by Priscar herself. May this book be an encouragement to those who seek to follow Jesus.

Jordan Bowler
Former Pastor, The Community Church, Sauchie - Scotland

Evangelist Priscar Manei has written a book that is long overdue in the Christian arena. Using sound Biblical references, she shows the reader how to recognize a calling from God, how to develop a servant's attitude, and the practical steps one must take in following that calling, regardless of the naysayers or well-meaning friends and family members who try to dissuade us from our ministry. The insights in this book will touch the reader's heart through the Holy Spirit and give hope to those who are questioning their call from God. Whether you are just starting out in your ministry, or are a life-long servant of God, the power of the Holy Spirit will shine through Priscar's words and guide you on your journey toward fulfilling God's purpose for your life. !

Jeanne Marie Leach
Christian Author, editor, and speaker - USA
www.jeannemarieleach.com

DEDICATION

I dedicate this book to my mother, Grace, who has gone home to be with the Lord.

Mum, you are my inspiration. I think about you all the time and keep wondering how you lived through all life's adversity. Your thoughts and teachings encourage me in difficult times. I love you Mum. You are the best mother ever in the world! I thank the Lord for having given me the opportunity to lead you to Him while on your deathbed. I was young in the Lord, and perhaps I should have said, "Rise in the name of Jesus." Anyway, the Lord knows best. I thank the Lord once again for opening your eyes to receive the vision that He has given me about my future and my service to Him. I will never forget your smile! Cheers, Mum!

Psalms 137:3-4 - For there those who carried us away captive asked of us a song, And those who plundered us requested mirth, Saying, "Sing us one of the songs of Zion!" How shall we sing the Lord's song in a foreign land?

GRATITUDE

I extend my deepest gratitude to all those who, in one way or another, did so much to help me achieve my potential in God. Special thanks to each one of you for doing all you could in providing for my basic needs when I needed them most. My tribute goes to this wonderful woman of God who after conducting the Easter Service I attended sometime ago while I was recuperating, came to me with encouraging words, saying "Since my children are not here to celebrate with me, I miss them, please take this money and buy yourself something." The Lord said, "What ever you do to these little ones, you have done it to me." The Lord will reward you all richly.! Thank you

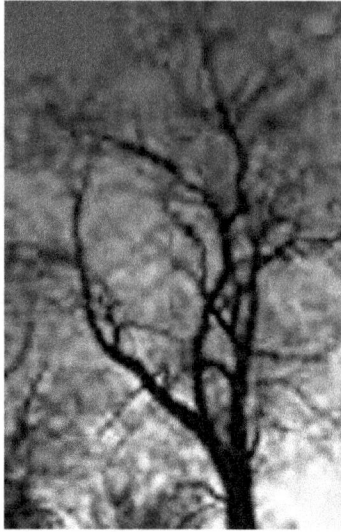

Micah 7:7-8 - Therefore I will look to the Lord; I will wait for the God of my salvation; My God will hear me. Do not rejoice over me, my enemy; when I fall, I will arise; when I sit in darkness, the Lord will be a light to me.

SPECIAL THANKS

I also extend my appreciation to Dr Thomas Manton IV for believing in me and for giving me the opportunity to serve and mature in God's calling. Dr. Manton never ceases to encourage me to pursue the call of God in my life. It was not easy starting out without much experience in ministry, but it was worth it. Thank you for being a good mentor.

I also thank every man and woman of God who spoke words of encouragement into my life.

Philippians 1:19 – For I know that this will turn out for my deliverance through your prayer and the supply of the Spirit of Jesus Christ

PREFACE

I never imagined I would ever write a book. It was therefore with utter surprise that I once received a prophecy through Dr Thomas Manton IV that I would do so. Initially, I just laughed it off. I did not see how that could be! Then one day I returned from a conference and thoughts began flooding my mind. I felt pressed in the spirit to put them down on paper. Within a week, the thumbnail sketch of this book was complete! I thank the Lord for having given me this opportunity. Thank you, Lord!

2 Corinthians 1:10-11 – who delivered us from so great a death, and does deliver us; in whom we trust that He will still deliver us, you also helping together in prayer for us, that thanks may be given by many persons on our behalf for the gift granted to us through many.

INTRODUCTION

They Went In and Came Out Victorious:

A Servant's Wilderness Experience

I trust this book will encourage all who are serving the Lord. It is my hope it will also benefit those Christians who "feel called" to be ministers but are unsure of how a calling unfolds or what it entails.

As a Christian, you have a spiritual gift. You may be wandering aimlessly or searching for what that gift might be. Or you believe you have a gift, but not sure how to embrace it. If you are not submissive to the proper spiritual authority, your gift will do no one much good. This book will help you understand the godly principles that can enable you to discover and begin exercising your gift.

Every Christian has a calling to some ministry, but many do not know how to exercise their godly given gifts. Others think they must attend a Bible college. God does not call everyone to Bible college or seminary, He does continue teaching and nurturing us for a lifetime.

God's training will adapt to you and it will not end until we see him in glory. Beware! God's school for the saints is tough, rife with hard knocks. Those with a high calling may also face significant opposition and vindictiveness from various sources. Constantly remind yourself of the following scriptures: *"For everyone to whom much is given, from him much will be required; and to whom much has been committed, of him they will ask the more,"* and *"Yet it shall not be so among you; but whoever desires to become great among you, let him be your servant." (Luke 12:48,* Matthew *20:26)*

Hard times will sometimes create doubt. You may begin to wonder whether God cares and whether He has called you to this place. This book will try to guide you through the hard times and seek to inspire you through your hardship and assuring you that God is faithful.

It is important to always bear in mind what the Word says in *Isaiah 43:2: "When you pass through the waters, I will be with you; And through the rivers, they shall not overflow you. When you walk through the fire, you shall not be burned, Nor shall the flame scorch you."*

Your "walk through the fire" may be synonymous with or proceeded by a "wilderness experience" designed to prepare you for your calling. Some people linger longer in the wilderness than they need to.

Others bypass the wilderness altogether. They leap right into ministry without waiting for God to finish preparing their "spiritual covers" (such as mentors or accountability partners). As a result they sometimes end up in the wrong ministry or the right ministry at the wrong time, and ultimately prove ineffective.

Know what and to whom you are designated by God to serve. I firmly believe in the laying on of hands to anoint with God's Spirit at the start of a ministry. The fruits of this connection will depend on what spirit is in each of those who lay hands on you. If you are truly prepared to begin your ministry, you will choose the right people to commission you, and you will not let "politeness" stop you from speaking out if you discern that something is wrong with the ordination. This book can help you develop the needed discernment.

Above all, I hope God will use this book to reveal to you His purpose for your life and what you must do to reach your destiny. Remember, you're calling and authority ultimately comes from God. Only God is the giver of eternal gifts, no human being can give another the call, no more than one human can create another. Even the wisest spiritual leaders are only vessels whom God uses to fulfill His plan. Do not; use this fact as an excuse for failing to respect your leaders. No call reaches full potential except through mentorship and service: there is no shortcut.

Finally, remember the Bible never has and never will change! It is the same Word, just as *"Jesus Christ is the same yesterday, today, and forever" (Hebrews 13:8).*

Psalms 80:1 – Give ear, O shepherd of Israel. You who lead Joseph like a flock; you who dwell between the cherubim, shine forth!

TABLE OF CONTENTS

Chapter One

What is True Servant hood?

In spiritual terms, servants are those focused on their God-ordained destiny. The biblical understanding of servants signifies those who are strong in faith and those who have given themselves freely to God's service. All truth is God's truth and we must dedicate ourselves to spreading that truth. We will then --become- love what we do because we will know the almighty God called us to our task.

Prophets were not the only ones referred to as servants in the Old Testament *(Malachi. 4:4)* Christ's coming was spoken prophetically and He was referred to as a servant of God *(Isaiah. 42:1, 19)*. Those who ministered to the prophets as Joshua did for Moses and Elisha did for Elijah were known as servants or assistants *(Exodus 24:13)*.

Of course there were also servants in the bible who were actually Israelite slaves. These kinds of servants were in bondage to a human master. *'As a hired servant and a sojourner he shall be with you, and shall serve you until the Year of Jubilee'* *(Leviticus 25:40)*. They were required to serve their masters for seven years and to be freed on the eighth year. *(Deuteronomy* 15:12) *"If your brother, a Hebrew man, or a Hebrew woman, is sold to you and serves you six years, then in the seventh year, you shall let him go free from you. (Deuteronomy 15:18). It shall not seem hard to you when you send him away free from you; for he hath been worth a double hired servant in serving you six years. Then the Lord your God will bless you in all that you do'.*

These slaves were given an option to stay in bondage. Their decision would then make them lifelong slaves. *(Deuteronomy 15:16-17).*

However, servants who served the Prophets in the Old Testament received the mantles and became Prophets after a successful completion of their assignment. *'He also took up the mantle of Elijah that had fallen from him, and went back and stood by the bank of the Jordan' (2 Kings 2:13).*

It is an honor to be referred to as a servant of God, a reference which deserves to be respected and treasured. Christ emphasizes that anyone desiring to be great in the Kingdom of God must become the least by serving. *"But he who is greatest among you shall be your servant" (Matthew 23:11).*

The New Testament has not changed the plan of God. On the contrary, the New Testament has been a tool to foster those who seek out a one-to-one relationship with God. Christ had twelve disciples in His inner circle and many more followed Him. Christ therefore, first explained his word to his disciples, and in turn, his word, and his teachings were conveyed by his disciples to the masses.

Jesus also said, "Most assuredly, I say to you, he who believes in Me, the works that I do he will do also; and greater works than these he will do, because I go to My Father (John 14:12). The Lord promised, 'You may do greater works than He did...' He later added another seventy disciples whom He

20

commissioned two by two *'After these things the Lord appointed seventy others also,* and sent them two by two before His face into every city and place where He Himself was about to go' (Luke 10:1).*

To some, the tasks the Lord asked of them was menial. In one case, He instructed his disciples to go to a town where they would find a common animal. *He said, "Go into the village opposite you, and immediately you will find a donkey tied, and a colt with her. Loose them and bring them to Me. (Matthew 21:2)*

In another case, The Lord asked them to go to an inn to inform a man He would like to celebrate the Jewish ceremony in his house: *"And He said, 'Go into the city to a certain man, and say to him, 'The Teacher says, "My time is at hand; I will keep the Passover at your house with My disciples"' (Matthew 26:18).*

The Lord instructed Peter to go and retrieve a coin from a fish's mouth so they could pay their tax. *(See Matthew 17:24 – 27)*. These examples clearly show that the disciples were not just with the Lord in his mass meetings and healing sessions, but they also did physical and sometime menial work to facilitate the Lord's ministry on earth. In this regard disciples had to experience the practical side of ministry while at the same time acquiring their spiritual knowledge.

Contact with the multitudes that flocked to hear the word and teachings of Jesus was useful to the disciples, they too served at the same time *(Matthew 14:15-21)*. They were included in every aspect of Christ's ministry.

They did not have a badly informed mind-set. They genuinely loved the Lord and the people. They wanted Jesus to have a positive impact on the congregation as he had in their lives.

In the early days of spiritual growth, servants of Christ are usually enmeshed in many battles. The devil tries to obstruct their spiritual destiny. Thus, servants know when they have arrived to the place of assignment. Humility in their performance is one way of knowing whether the character is forming into godliness. They do not easily give in to intimidation. These people are consumed with the zeal of the Lord *'Because zeal for Your house has eaten me up, And the reproaches of those who reproach You have fallen on me' - Psalms 69:9.* Therefore the said persons are selfless as far as God's work is concerned and, in turn, they trust God to solve any complications that may arise as a result of their commitment to His work.

My mentor taught me the Lord absolves crises. God will find a safe path. Take this knowledge to heart. As a true servant your efforts will succeed despite the obstacles you encounter on your journey.

At this point it may be necessary to look at the phrase servant to understand what I mean when this term is used.

The term servant when associated in this context has been repackaged. Some Churches use different expressions, which amounts to the same.

'Protégé' or 'PA – Personal Assistant' are common expressions used in modern churches or ministries. In biblical context 'Servant or 'Assistant' were the general used references. Having done some researches we came up with the following meanings:

PROTÉGÉ
One who is protected or trained or whose career is furthered by a person of experience, prominence, or influence

SERVANT
One that serves, others common term referring to public servants or domestic workers; especially one that performs duties about the person or home of a master or personal employer

PERSONAL ASSISTANT
Someone employed to perform secretarial and administrative tasks for somebody such as an executive who has many responsibilities.

In the biblical function: A servant is one who works through the guidance of a prophet, in a similar way disciples were guided by Christ, wages was not the main focus.

A servant will have their individual needs met by their masters. They are completely dependant on their masters for their survival.

If a person applies for a vocational position in the church or ministry, it can be considered that the individual is working in a godly environment. While a servant divinely manifest in their place of assignment. A servant's income depends upon the income of the ministry or church and can be given to the individual concerned in any time frame. It is up to the men and women of God to bear in mind that servants have needs. Such needs are part of modern living. These necessitates may include a roof over ones head, and food and clothing. Without such basic needs it will not be easy to serve even as a volunteer.

There are now cases today where servants obtain part-time work in order to meet their expense while continuing their voluntary contribution to God.

However, lay servants are not dependent upon wages. They seek   anointing or "mantle" for service. Masters should understand that the servants require to be looked after in order to meet their basic needs.

A servant is chosen as part of God's plan. Note, in most cases, a servant may serve many "internships". In recent times one may find themselves being called to a different ministry, or to a number of ministries. Worry not if you are called to attend a number of ministries. Submit yourself to God's will. And when the time comes, God will promote you.

The following, are the qualities needed for one to become a useful servant.

- A servant should be a prayerful person with ability to intercede, thus mediating in prayer on behalf of others.

24

- A good servant understands the importance of being a worshipper of God.

- In most cases, servants have been perceived to be humble people. They understand that they have been called to give freely of themselves.

- A good trait for servants to possess is compassion. We see this characteristic demonstrated when Gehazi, the servant of Elisha, mentioned to him that the Shunamitte woman had no child.

- A servant is loyal to his master and would not entertain any gossip or idol speech.

- Servants are also peacemakers.

Deuteronomy 3:22 – Teach me Your way, O Lord; I will walk in Your truth; Unite my heart to fear Your name.

Chapter Two

Jewels in the Kingdom
Compassionate Rescuers

When I think of jewels I am reminded of special kind of people. Individual who have undertaken all they can to assist spread the Gospel of Jesus Christ. Future chapters will reveal human gems who have served biblical leaders. This chapter will focus on the 'jewels' God brought into my own life.

I want to take a moment to remember the people who have placed their lives at risk to help others. I want to borrow just a few seconds of your time and ask you to spare a thought for the individuals who took the Good News to harsh places such as China and other troubled parts of the world. They risked their lives because they are determined to let others know, *"For God so loved the world that He gave His only begotten Son, that whoever believes in Him should not perish, but have everlasting life."* *(John 3:16)* These individuals assist in menial ways which enable God-given assignments run smoothly. They do not complain; they are willing to work any time.

I was once advised to first look after myself and not waste time with the men and women of God.

"What have you got to show for yourself?" he quizzed me.

His advice did not concern me. To some I may appear of humble means. I knew then, as I know now what had God instilled in me. Some may judge on superficial appearance, but God's eyes are deeper. He searches our hearts and our motives, and then He decides our destinies.

Another suggested I turn my mind to more material things and marriage. But when I meditate on the scriptures, Christ Himself says, *"He who finds his life will lose it, and he who loses his life for My sake will find it" (Matthew 10:39).*

People in our lives, even the ones we respect, can lead us astray and away from the truth. By studying the Word of God, we can never be led away from God's reality.

You may remember the story of a man of God sent from Judah to Bethel to proclaim the Word of God? The story can be found in 1 Kings 13:1-22. He was instructed by the Lord not to return home the same way he traveled but he disobeyed. On his way home, he met an older prophet who convinced him to go back the same way he came, though the Lord forbade him. He was murdered on the very road forbidden to him by the Lord. The elder mislead him, but he trusted him because he was thought to be a man of God.

The person who challenged my personal life was also considered to be a man of God. I reflect had I took his advice believing he would help me fulfill my dreams; I would have been following a wrong path. It is our responsibility to listen to the Holy Spirit. Aligning ourselves with the Word of God could save us a great deal.

28

In the year 2005, I fell ill. I was unaware what was wrong with me; I lived with the illness for about two years before I was finally admitted into the hospital. Since my childhood, God had blessed me with good health. During this time of illness, I kept telling myself, I would soon get better, but for over a year, I hard severe back pains.

Finally, I went to see a doctor at an emergency clinic. He examined my back and gave me a clean bill of health. He could see no problem and assured me I had nothing to worry about. He prescribed painkillers and sent me home. I took the painkillers as instructed, but there was no improvement. I did not wish to be taking painkillers indefinitely, so I consulted a different doctor.

She too offered pain killers, and then asked me to return in ten days if I did not feel better. Fourteen days passed with no improvement. I returned to my new woman doctor. After an examination she concluded she was unable to treat me herself. She did however, refer me to a Hospital.

I was examined by more doctors and eventually informed that I had spinal tuberculosis. From the moment they discovered my conditioned I was not allowed to walk and I was confined to a hospital bed for 42 days.

Drugs could not ease the unbearable pain in my lungs. There were times when I could not turn from one side to another because of the pain. I took comfort in the: verse: *"I can do all things through Christ who strengthens me."* Only then would I gain the strength to turn my body.

All who shared my hospital ward soon learnt I was a devout Christian. At times I would ask the nurses who were also Christians to pray for me. They did. I underwent spinal surgery, which proved successful. My recover was such that it impressed all the doctors. I ask this of you, if God can be for you, who then can be against you? I am amazed by the love of God. The Lord promised to be with us always. *Hebrew 13:5 says, "Let your conduct be without covetousness; be content with such as you have. For the Lord says, 'I will never leave you nor forsake you.'"* God proved His love to me.

As I mentioned my doctor was impressed with my healing. I thank God for guiding his hands to perform such a skilled operation. He is an accomplished man of few words. While I lay there in the hospital, the doctors thought the operation would take a whole day. They were not sure what to expect, and I grew nervous when I heard this. Intercession on my behalf was offered in different parts of the world. People prayed for me to have a quick and speedy recovery.

My mentor prayed endlessly and asked believers to intercede. As I saw the love of God and I relaxed and looked forward to the operation. A bed was made ready for me at the HDU (High Dependence Unit). It was an indication the surgeon was anticipating complications after my surgery.

I was informed that during the operation my surgeon was laboring in silence and at a point, part of the theater equipment fell. Another was ordered from a neighboring hospital.

As I opened my eyes I could hear them calling my name. Doctors and nurses stood on both sides of my hospital bed. They actually clapped with joy when I first opened my eyes.

"The operation was successful," one said while another commented, "Even the Doctor is smiling."

Two weeks later my doctor came to see me in the hospital room. He was quite surprised to find me seated in a chair.

"Look at you!" he exclaimed. "How are your legs?"

"They are fine, doctor."

"At least you are not paralyzed!"

Although I was weak, my heart leaped for joy. "Look, doctor," I said. "I can move around, and I can bend a little."

"You need not be here anymore," he told me, a huge smile on his face. "You have been here long enough. You need to go home for a change of environment."

With these words of assurance, I was discharged to go home. In total I was hospitalized for fifty days.

After the hospital stay, I received mixed reactions from those who think they know the mind of God and have answers for everything. Some said I had been used as a slave when referring to my service in the work of God. But my involvement in these ministries had been prophetically spoken.

My response was then, and always is, "What were my motives while serving in those ministries? Was I serving to please man or to please my God? What were my expectations? Would God discount my labor of love towards Him? I do not think so. Human beings are only vessels whom God uses to fulfill His plan for us.

While my mentor was away, the Lord led me divinely to the fellowship of a certain man of God where I received spiritual support, and I got back on my feet again after several visits. This man of God prophesied life into me even when all seemed gone. At my lowest point in life, he could visualize me speaking the Word of God to many people. He is a humble man of God, who is careful not to take credit from God. I thank God for his family, his wife, his ministry team, and the congregation in general.

I once met another man of God who started conversing with me. After a while he said, "You know, the Holy Spirit prompted me to give you this money." He handed me some cash. From time to time people who came to see me handed me money, each time saying the Lord told them to do it. These unexpected actions came to me at exactly the right time. It was at a period of my life when I was at my lowest ebb. God has always proved faithful to those who are faithful to Him. Thank you, Lord!

While serving God we need to be careful of those who speak negatively to discourage us. They manipulate our circumstances to their advantage. Some are messengers of the devil, masquerading as angels of light. They find ways to limit the blessings God has for us.

Some have said I have been used and manipulated by ministry leaders. That may be true. I suppose we could also say that Joshua was used by Moses, Elisha was used by Elijah, the disciples were used by Christ, and Timothy was used by Paul. So it would be with every other person who was chosen by God to serve.

I was once told I was experiencing a generational curse. We read in *John 9: 1-7*, *"Now as Jesus passed by, He saw a man who was blind from birth. And His disciples asked Him, saying, 'Rabbi, who sinned, this man or his parents, that he was born blind?' Jesus answered, 'Neither this man nor his parents sinned, but that the works of God should be revealed in him. I must work the works of Him who sent Me while it is day; the night is coming when no one can work. As long as I am in the world, I am the light of the world.'" When He had said these things, He spat on the ground and made clay with the saliva; and He anointed the eyes of the blind man with the clay. And He said to him, 'Go, wash in the pool of Siloam' (which is translated, Sent). So he went and washed, and came back seeing."*

Only God has the answers when we fail to understand why certain things happen the way they do. There are circumstances in one's life which could be caused by a generational curse, and some may not be. We need not draw conclusions for every case, trying to make ourselves experts in the things of God. The point I am trying to make is a simple one. Not every mishap we encounter is a result of generational curse.

It is my sincere hope that you will be encouraged to keep pursuing the call God has for you with the understanding persecution also comes with it. I pray you will eventually overcome the hardships you are going through and become a testimony to other people.

The Lord responded to the disciples' question that the man's blindness was not because the man or his parents sinned, but that the glory of God may be seen through him.

I do not deny that generational curses exist. But some have labeled every negative situation in their lives in this way. I believe Christ became a curse on our behalf when He died at Calvary. Therefore, when one is born again, the person renounces the past and becomes a new individual in Christ.

There is a mighty woman of God, whom God is using powerfully throughout the world today. A number of years ago she discovered she had breast cancer. This happened while she was already in the ministry, and God was moving impressively through her. Could it be said that this woman was suffering because of a generational curse?

Mark 10: 29 – 31 So Jesus answered and said, "Assuredly, I say to you, there is no one who has left house or brothers or sisters or father or mother or wife or children or lands, for My sake and the gospel's, who shall not receive a hundredfold now in this time--houses and brothers and sisters and mothers and children and lands, with persecutions--and in the age to come, eternal life. But many who are first will be last, and the last first."

The Lord made it clear that those who give up what they have to serve Him will be blessed. God detailed that a righteous man will be awarded for good deeds, and a sinful man will be judged. Ezekiel, chapter 18 tells us that if a righteous man begets a son who lives sinfully, the righteous man will be awarded for his own deeds. And if the sinful son begets a son who lives righteously, the son will be awarded for his own good deeds, not for his father's lack of them.

"If he has walked in My statutes and kept My judgments faithfully--He is just; He shall surely live!" says the Lord God" *(Ezekiel 18:9).* This is what the chapter has to say about a son leading a sinful life. *"If he has exacted usury or taken increase, shall he then live? He shall not live! If he has done any of these abominations, He shall surely die; His blood shall be upon him"* *(Ezekiel 18:13).*

And when this sinful son begets a son who ends up living a righteous life, the son who is the grandson of the first man, he will also be rewarded. *Ezekiel 18:17 says, "Who has withdrawn his hand from the poor and not received usury or increase, but has executed My judgments and walked in My statutes-- he shall not die for the iniquity of his father; he shall surely live!"*

God did not promise us a trouble-free life. He made it clear persecution will be part of earthly life until we reach eternal life. Many people have had wrong inclination toward those who are paying a price as result of poor knowledge of the contents of the Bible. Such people want blessings, not prepared to undertake what is necessary to receive them. They want the soft side of the Gospel, but refuse to take the hard side of it. The Gospel comes with both sides.

Some wonder, *"Why have I been serving God faithfully and am still going through this?* Or, *"If I am under a cover, then I should not be going through trials."*

The apostle Paul served God faithfully and helped pioneer the apostolic movement. He had a servant named Timothy, who had stomach problems and other illnesses. Paul reminded Timothy, when writing him, to take something for his stomach *(See 1 Timothy 5:23)*. Throughout the Apostle Paul's Christian service, he also faced much physical suffering and persecution. He detailed them clearly in his letter as shown in the scripture below.

"Are they ministers of Christ?--I speak as a fool--I am more: in labors more abundant, in stripes above measure, in prisons more frequently, in deaths often. From the Jews five times I received forty stripes minus one. Three times I was beaten with rods; once I was stoned; three times I was shipwrecked; a night and a day I have been in the deep; in journeys often, in perils of waters, in perils of robbers, in perils of my own countrymen, in perils of the Gentiles, in perils in the city, in perils in the wilderness, in perils in the sea, in perils among false brethren; in weariness and toil, in sleeplessness often, in hunger and thirst, in fasting often, in cold and nakedness-- besides the other things, what comes upon me daily: my deep concern for all the churches" (2 Corinthians 11:23-28).

Would it be right to imply that Timothy was not under spiritual cover? Or was the apostle Paul's anointing not enough to provide a spiritual cover? Questions like these may forever remain a mystery to us.

We need to put our trust in God and find satisfaction in Him, rather than trying to find answers to every incident in our lives. If we are not careful, we could be misled. If the apostle Paul had lived in our time, people would have come up with many explanations for his infirmities. Note that in Paul's letter to Timothy, he mentioned that Timothy had other ailments. These two were true servants of God. Why did they have to go through such things? Paul mentioned a thorn in his flesh which could have caused some form of sickness. Whatever it was, Paul remained faithful in serving God.

It is unfortunate some may offer you help with ill motive. Such people want to take credit and seeking recognition. How can one claim to love and have an indifference or selfish nature? One characteristic will betray the other.

When I received a United Kingdom visa, and before leaving my country Kenya, I went to thank the ladies who had prayed for me. I was surprised when they said; "Let us thank the Lord for what He has done." We held hands and stood in a circle. Their prayer shocked me, but I was in agreement with them. I must say, though, I did not fully understanding what I was agreeing to. Nevertheless, their simple prayer proved to be powerful in the years that followed. I have come to understand that God used them to begin His purpose in my life.

Quote from their prayer "Father we thank you for giving your daughter the United Kingdom visa. We are now sending her over as your servant in that land, protect her in Jesus name." Through these fellow servants, God mapped out His will for me.

While coping with the loss of my mother, her friends have been kind to my siblings and I.

I do have fond memories of these ladies who have played key roles in our lives. One gave me helpful advice, which proved very helpful in ushering me to my new destiny.

Two of these women are currently in the United Kingdom. They do however, return to Kenya regularly. They have a special place in my heart.

In the beginning when God was introducing me to ministry, He took me to several places and shifted me as He saw fit in order to have His purposed fulfilled, not forgetting that He does not share His glory with any other. There a time a group of ladies and I stayed at a young woman's house. Despite being a single mother she allowed us to live with her. It was a fulfilling experience. We spent most of our time in intercession. This was a time which proved to be one of the uplifting moments in my life. I thank God for this woman's love to have opened her house to us. Soon after, a certain woman of God invited me to live with her and her family for several months. I later moved out and since then we have remained in touch.

When word got to her about my illness, she came to see me at the hospital. When I returned home, she and her friend bought for me groceries. Thereafter she cooked for me until I was strong enough to tend to myself. She told me I should never allow myself to feel alone. I should remember, she told me, I have Sisters in Christ that I can call on when I am in need. To this very day my Sisters in Christ keep a constant vigil eye on me.

Another woman had no steady employment. She was going through a difficult time, but her circumstances did not hinder her from coming to see me almost every day. She prayed for me, brought fruit, drinks, Christian materials, and an audio Bible. She did it out of love for Christ. When I think of the way God has used this lady in my life, tears flow down my cheeks. After I left the hospital, she phoned me often to find out how I was feeling. She barely had enough money for transportation, and I can testify to that, yet she never complained or mistreated me in any way.

In the early days after leaving the hospital, I could not do anything for myself. Whenever she came around, she helped me get dressed. She made me experience Christ's love through her. It is my prayer that God will bless her. Her labor has borne witness to me and to the Lord of her love for Christ. I remember and thank all who helped and prayed for me during this season in my life.

These individuals did all they could, including relentless prayer, to ensure that I was getting back to normal. They shed tears and spoke victory over me. A few months later, when one of the ladies who brought groceries saw me looking better, she said, "Thank you, Lord, this is the Priscar that I knew."

That is why when I think about jewels in the Kingdom of God, I think about these people and others worldwide. I think about those who dedicate their lives to spread God's love. They serve in different capacities in ministries and in churches to ensure that the work of God runs smoothly. These people are unique and few. They are precious jewels whom we need to treasure. *"They shall be Mine," says the Lord of hosts, "On the day that I make them My jewels. And I will spare them As a man spares his own son who serves him." Malachi 3:17*

Chapter Three

Value Divine Visitations
Making a Covenant with God

Genesis 28:13-15 says "And behold, the Lord stood above it and said: 'I am the Lord God of Abraham your father and the God of Isaac; the land on which you lie I will give to you and your descendants. Also your descendants shall be as the dust of the earth; you shall spread abroad to the west and the east, to the north and the south; and in you and in your seed all the families of the earth shall be blessed. Behold, I am with you and will keep you wherever you go, and will bring you back to this land; for I will not leave you until I have done what I have spoken to you.'"

Using Jacob as an illustration, According to research, Jacob is derived from late Latin *Iacobus,* from Greek *Iakobos,* from Hebrew *Yagob, yaagov, Yaăqō).* It is a spoken name, referring to the circumstances of Jacob's birth, meaning "holds the heel." He was named so because he held onto the heel of his twin brother, Esau, at birth. The name is the same as James (Greek version), the son of Zebedee who later became an apostle

The Lord declared to Jacob the vision He had shown to his father, Abraham, that He would give the land to them. He assured Jacob He would protect him. The Bible states one's destiny is ordained before birth. Jacob inherited the promise given to Abraham and Isaac about how their descendants would inherit the Promised Land. However, Jacob went away to some form of 'wilderness' running away from his brother Essau.

The wilderness is not a joyful place to be. It is full of undesirable experiences and hardship. There are so many battles to fight, but the outcome is victory for those who have put their trust in the Lord.

Nebuchadnezzar spoke, saying to them, "Is it true, Shadrach, Meshach, and Abed-Nego, that you do not serve my gods or worship the gold image which I have set up? Now if you are ready at the time you hear the sound of the horn, flute, harp, lyre, and psaltery, in symphony with all kinds of music, and you fall down and worship the image which I have made, good! But if you do not worship, you shall be cast immediately into the midst of a burning fiery furnace. And who is the god who will deliver you from my hands?" Shadrach, Meshach, and Abed-Nego answered and said to the king, "O Nebuchadnezzar, we have no need to answer you in this matter. If that is the case, our God whom we serve is able to deliver us from the burning fiery furnace, and He will deliver us from your hand, O king. But if not, let it be known to you, O king, that we do not serve your gods, nor will we worship the gold image which you have set up." (Daniel 3:14-18)

It is both comforting and encouraging to know that God has already assured us of His protection. Shadrach, Meshach and Abed-Nego were confident that God will deliver them. They were not intimidated by King Nebuchadnezzar or his threats. They told Nebuchadnezzar that their God will deliver them and if not they will still continue to worship Him. We go through so much, yet few seem willing to help. Family and friends may desert us, because, to them, the book of our lives is as good as done.

Perhaps you used to go out with them, receiving many phone calls from them each week to discuss what to do together on the weekend. Now you find out through other people these "loyal" friends are avoiding you.

These are times to remember the promises of God given to you either in a vision, dream, or through His servant. God will fulfill His Word. I suggest you stop moaning about your hardships. Keep your focus toward the goal. Isaiah 43 reveals that God is with us at all times. You, too, will come out of this with great victory. This is a temporary season in preparation for the assignment God has for you! The vision will come to pass; it may tarry, but it will come to pass.

Jacob could identify his place of visitation: the place in which he wrestled with God to gain His blessing and enter, in effect, a gateway of heaven. While in this wilderness season, it is important to pray that God will both keep you and broaden your understanding. Trusting God to be in the right place at the right time will improve your confidence *(Proverbs 3:5-6)*.

This can be achieved through intensive prayer. Divine encounters occur when you are in the right place with God at the right time. The Holy Spirit is there to lead you if you will allow Him. Jacob made a covenant at Bethel and vowed to the Lord, if God would keep him through the wilderness, He would be his God. This is an impressive eye-opener.

A covenant helps to initiate God's help in difficult times or when we have a desperate want or need. Jacob made a covenant with the Lord, because he knew God honors covenants. He knew it would take a solid promise from God to see him through the wilderness.

Jacob was aware the time would come when he would lack the daily needs of life, such as food and clothing, and he would have to depend on God for his daily bread. This experience is common to those called to serve God, through it they develop faith and total dependence on the Lord. And God reminds us: *"Let your conduct be without covetousness; be content with such as you have. For He Himself has said, "I will never leave you nor forsake you" (Hebrews 13:5)*. God provides for the vision; he is Jehovah Jireh, the provider.

"So Jacob went on his journey and came to the land of the people of the East. And he looked, and saw a well in the field; and behold, there were three flocks of sheep lying by it; for out of that well they watered the flocks. A large stone was on the well's mouth. Now all the flocks would be gathered there; and they would roll the stone from the well's mouth, water the sheep, and put the stone back in its place on the well's mouth. And Jacob said to them, 'My brethren, where are you from?' And they said, 'We are from Haran.' Then he said to them, 'Do you know Laban the son of Nahor?' And they said, 'We know him.' So he said to them, 'Is he well?' And they said, 'He is well. And look, his daughter Rachel is coming with the sheep." (Genesis 29:1-6).

When Jacob started his journey through the wilderness after his encounter with the Lord at Bethel, the Spirit of the Lord led him to the place of his assignment. After finding his uncle's home, he was told that Rachel,

Laban's daughter, whom he would come to love, was on the way. At that point Jacob did not know what assignment awaited him at Laban's place.

Sometimes we come across individuals who wonder about their calling, and who want someone to give them an answer. They do not know to whom they are assigned! Neither did Jacob know he would be serving Laban. However, he allowed God to order his footsteps.

We often forget the Lord will show us the way. Lack of understanding and proper knowledge contributes to premature beginnings. Sadly, these kinds of people remain in the wilderness; they fail to reach their full potential because of ignorance or rebellion. There is power in being humble. The Bible says, *"Blessed are the meek, for they shall inherit the earth" (Matthew 5:5).*

Jacob was ready to serve. He immediately recognized his place of assignment and did not waste time. When Jacob saw Rachel, he rolled the stone from the well's mouth and gave the flock of Laban water to drink *(Genesis 29:10).* A servant does not wonder whether he should serve, but he gets on with it. Jacob did not ask Rachel whether he should water the sheep; he just did it.

Assignments can also be in a difficult location physically or spiritually. But to whom much is given, much is required. The level of your calling is sometimes determined by the toughest battle you must fight. Laban gave a warm welcome to Jacob, not knowing the same man would be his son-in-law, and he would betray the young man many times in their future together *(Genesis 29: 14-30)*.

Occasionally, we encounter parables in the Bible of how an enemy will use a master to frustrate a servant. This causes setbacks or delay in the servant's calling.

Jacob served Laban for fourteen years to get his prize – Rachel. Laban probably did not realize he was meant to humble a proud, deceptive Jacob with his own arrogance. He asked Jacob what his wages would be but then cut the wages ten times.

Victory does not come without a fight. Jacob had to serve for fourteen years to marry Rachel. David is also an individual who earned respect from the Israelites when he acted humbly no matter how Saul abused him. God will give us the desires of our heart if they meet His requirement. (according to 1 John 3:22) This is a time when one envisions and "prays through" the obstacles that are being cast across one's path.

Laban deceived Jacob. He gave him Leah as his bride instead of Rachel whom he loved. Laban's deception did not stop Jacob's love to Rachel he chose to serve seven more years so he could marry her. But God is not a deceptive master. Imagine what gifts God can give to those who yearn to serve Him? Can you imagine how anointed and blessed they would be?

Material things of this world will pass away, but the good we do for God in the name of Jesus will last forever.

Every promotion comes with opposition, and every success in life arrives through hard work. Christians face spiritual battles that may hinder them from reaching their destiny, but if we stand firm in Christ, we will end up victorious. Jacob refused to give in to the enemy. He patiently agreed to serve Laban for another seven years.

It is paramount to have honesty and integrity while serving a man or woman of God. You should not walk away from your place of assignment without giving proper notice unless you have been forced to do so by extraordinary events. One does not leave until God permits it. Old Testament scripture states that a slave must be freed on the seventh year, and only he or she can decide to go or to stay. It also states if the person stays, he will become a slave forever. Just as God rested on the seventh day after the creation, so is the servant to be freed.

If your master requests an extension of your service, as in Jacob's case, then you need to pray, fast, and think clearly so you may act suitably. Do not forget, the enemy tried to distract Jacob from his blessings. It was through Rachel that Joseph was born, and Joseph was the rare individual God used to preserve the Hebrews in Egypt during the famine period. This would not have happened if Jacob had not demonstrated patience. Being humble and maintaining the ability to exercise patience, is the best weapon you can use to fight the enemy. Toward the end of this story, we see that Jacob asked again to be released after serving Laban for the second seven-year term.

"Give me my wives and my children for whom I have served you, and let me go; for you know my service which I have done for you." And Laban said to him, 'Please stay, if I have found favor in your eyes, for I have learned by experience that the Lord has blessed me for your sake'" (Genesis 30:26-27). It is a servant's purpose to help his master achieve higher goals, and Jacob fulfilled his function well.

Theoretically, Laban could not deny Jacob his wish to leave. He noted Jacob was the source of his blessing, and admitted to Jacob it was through him he experienced great increase. Therefore he did not want to allow Jacob to move on in God's plan for him.

Laban admitted he was blessed because of Jacob's presence in his family, but Laban did not return blessing for blessing. Instead, he tried to profit at Jacob's expense in every possible way. Laban's sons also became jealous of Jacob's blessings. In spite of all, God was with Jacob and allowed no harm to come to him *(See Genesis 31:1).*

It is essential for everyone in ministry to remember they are not servants of men, but of God. Therefore, the reward comes from God. It is also important for leaders to treat those who are serving them as Christ treated His disciples. Instead of taking advantage and lording it over a support team, leaders should be kind and gracious, for they, also, are called to be servants of those who serve them

We should appreciate mentors who fulfill the will of God toward their protégés. A good mentor provides gracious leadership, and forms servants who are an asset for

God's Kingdom in the generation to come. Bible students should also not take for granted the fact Jacob was submissive to his mentor. Nor should we forget that he was deceived many times. Despite this, he remained faithful. Jacob worked hard for Laban, but Laban's sons did not see it that way. They were dominated by a critical spirit.

The wilderness experience is a rough journey in which only the strong survive. I can well remember my own struggles, and I recall wondering how long I would have to suffer.

I had a good job back home in Nairobi, Kenya, yet the Lord instructed me to resign. He appeared in a vision while I was sleeping, revealing to me the interview which I would have the next day with my employer.

At the actual interview the following day, they tried to convince me not to leave the organization. It was a good job, and I loved it. They offered many tempting packages. I almost gave in, but the only thing that kept me from saying yes was the vision I had the night before. The Lord had shown me the set up of the meeting---even the conversation, so I was well prepared for the conference. He commanded me not to give in to my employer. This proved difficult to do, but I had to obey the Lord.

Just before I went to collect my visa the following morning at the High Commission in Nairobi, the Lord appeared again and said to me, "Do not forget, it is I who is sending you to that land." I did not understand what He was trying to say to me, but these words never left my mind.

Then, when I moved to London, I went through much hardship. There was no one for me to lean on; I could only cry out to the Lord and remind Him of his promises. As time went by, His words began to make sense. He saved me spiritually and physically, and He preserved me in times when I thought I might even lose my life. These experiences, both bad and good, have become part of the ministry the Lord has for me. I look into the future and am grateful to Him. He is a much better employer than any human!

Be encouraged; in whatever circumstance you find yourself, there is a bright future ahead. I can give testimony to this. God knew my situations better than I. He took me to a place where there were no relatives to turn to for help so I could fully focus on Him. This would not have happened if I were in my own country! There would have been so many friends and relatives available ready to rescue me. Some would have discouraged me--with good intentions of course--but that would not have been the case in the eyes of God.

While in this season in your life, it is important to spend time in prayer and fasting in order to equip yourself to fight back with the Word of God. Do not forget; there is nothing new to the Lord concerning your circumstance. He desires for you to come out victorious. The scripture below is applicable during this season.

"Be strong and of good courage, do not fear nor be afraid of them; for the Lord your God, He is the One who goes with you. He will not leave you nor forsake you" (Deuteronomy 31:6).

The time for Jacob to reach out for his destiny finally arrived. The sons of Laban began to worry Jacob was taking away their father's belongings. It is so amazing, because, apart from this occasion, we do not read much of Laban's sons. On the other hand, Jacob understood that Laban's expression was not toward him as before – it was jealousy consuming the family. They might have wondered why Jacob was so blessed. Or why he should be allowed to leave with all that wealth? Jacob had a covenant with God; they did not. *"And Jacob said to them, 'I see your father's countenance, that it is not favorable toward me as before; but the God of my father has been with me. And you know that with all my might I have served your father. Yet your father has deceived me and changed my wages ten times, but God did not allow him to hurt me"* (Genesis 31:5 - 7). Jacob had started out as a rascal and deceiver; now we find him receiving a heavy dose of his own medicine.

Christians are often critical of one another. Then, surprisingly, we later find the accusers doing exactly the same thing. Jacob had lived a life of treachery; now he was on the receiving end of such treatment. We feel sorry for ourselves at times until we realize that we are reaping from those around us just what we have been handing out for years. Instead of embracing each other with the love of Christ we are always sniping at each other. It is surprising that even while we are in the wilderness, some believers strive with one another through spiritual jealousy and competition. Is there an end to the wilderness experience? We need to cling tightly to Christ to overcome these experiences in our daily lives.

Jacob told them that the God of his father was with him. Jacob's past vow to God at Bethel came to fulfillment after his desperate time in the wilderness.

"Then the Lord said to Jacob, 'Return to the land of your fathers and to your family, and I will be with you'" (Genesis 31:3). When we surrender ourselves to God, we need no longer worry because we have cast our cares upon Him. He takes charge of all that concerns us. As you read in the verse above, God came to Jacob's rescue. Jacob was ordered by God to go back to his homeland. After several challenges, he was confident God was with him and convinced through his experience God would rescue him from the wrath of Esau, his brother.

The trial you are going through today will not destroy you, but will make you into a stronger person. Put all your trust in God, and lean not on your own understanding.

"Now Jacob dwelt in the land where his father was a stranger, in the land of Canaan" (Genesis 37:1). Jacob established a covenant with God and was able to reach God's destination for him. He made it to the Promised Land!

Chapter Four

Loyalty: a Stepping-Stone to Greatness
Great Heights through Faithfulness

The name Joseph can be translated from Hebrew as signifying "The Lord will increase/add." It originates from Hebrew and is recorded in the Hebrew Bible as יוֹסֵף. Standard Hebrew is Yosef. Tiberian Hebrew and Aramaic, Yôsēp. In Arabic, it is Yūsuf.

Being the son of Jacob's old age, Jacob loved Joseph supremely. This love toward him triggered feelings of intense jealousy from his brethren *(See Genesis 37:4)*. Jacob made Joseph a coat of many colors, which symbolized greatness. Though Joseph certainly could have handled his relationship with his brothers more wisely, it is true that he was chosen from his early childhood as the following scripture reveals:

"Now Joseph had a dream, and he told it to his brothers; and they hated him even more. So he said to them, 'Please hear this dream which I have dreamed: There we were, binding sheaves in the field. Then behold, my sheaf arose and also stood upright; and indeed your sheaves stood all around and bowed down to my sheaf.' And his brothers said to him, 'Shall you indeed reign over us? Or shall you indeed have dominion over us?' So they hated him even more for his dreams and for his words'" (Genesis 37:5-8).

As we read this, we can fully understand Joseph's brothers were jealous of him. They did not want to accept Joseph's dreams. Yet God chose Joseph and planned his destiny specifically for the survival of God's chosen people.

Joseph later had another dream *(Genesis 37:9-11)*, and he told it to his brothers: this time the sun, the moon, and the eleven stars were bowing down to him. Joseph's second dream was sharp like a knife, and it pierced their hearts. They hated him more and began plotting how they would harm him. In this circumstance, it became obvious evil forces were working to cause great unrest between Joseph and his brothers. The devil thought that he had put a stop to Joseph's dream, but God overturned the evil to help Joseph reach his destiny.

His brothers hated him so much that they sold him as a slave. Joseph's wilderness experience proved a vital preparation for his post in Egypt as a chosen leader. They did not know they were making his dream become reality. Their evil scheme became a ladder for Joseph's destiny. In Egypt Joseph went through many struggles, and being in prison was just a part of it. He went through various experiences which I would refer to as different phases in the wilderness. Whenever it seemed as if he was making progress, something else appeared to halt his progress. Joseph won many battles, and he became a strategic leader in the Egyptian government. This would not have happened had he not been obedient to God and kept himself holy. God was with him. He had no time to plot evil against other people. He was busy and trusted God to reveal his dream.

54

Joseph went through three wilderness phases: His first phase began when his father's love and preference of him caused his brothers to isolate him. This must have been lonely for Joseph. However negative this appeared, it was for his good. God prepared him for his assignment in Egypt. He would have missed his family had he not experienced loneliness while with them.

We need to draw our faith from the Word of God to triumph over the obstacles the enemy sends our way. However ugly life becomes, unless we put our trust in God, we will never know what victory feels like. If Joseph had been comfortable at home, he would not have had the strength to carry on in Egypt. Our loved ones can make it too comfortable for us and cause us to miss our blessing. As a result, it could jeopardize our future effectiveness in what God wants to do through us

Except for Joseph's father and his kid brother, Benjamin, there was not much love for Joseph back home. His father rebuked him about the dream, yet he still pondered the matter in his mind. Joseph's life at home helped him adapt to his new life in the foreign land.

His second phase in the wilderness began when Joseph shared his dream with the family, and it provoked jealousy from his brothers. They plotted to kill him, but Joseph was blessed when Reuben, his elder brother, came to his rescue. Rather than suffer murder, Joseph was sold to the Egyptians as a slave.

When Joseph's brothers saw him coming from afar they began to plot against him. *Genesis 37:21-22* tells us how Reuben pleaded with them not to kill Joseph, but to cast him in a pit instead! God will always make a way out of danger for you. God will reward you for all the pain you have endured. Joseph eventually became a great leader in Egypt. This would not have been possible if he had allowed negative situations to put him down. The blessings of the Lord were in every place, all because of Josephs' presence in the Egyptian family *(See Genesis 39:5)*. However, I must not get ahead of myself.

"And Reuben said to them, 'Shed no blood, but cast him into this pit which is in the wilderness, and do not lay a hand on him"--that he might deliver him out of their hands, and bring him back to his father'" (Genesis 37:22).

Reuben saved Joseph from being killed by the brothers, hoping to return him to his father.

Some of you reading this book would have experienced rejection in your lives. You probably have lost self confidence in your self because of what you have gone through. I want you now to try and imagine what Joseph's own family had put him through. Though Joseph was admittedly arrogant, his family should have loved him regardless. Visualize in your mind what Joseph endured, but yet he emerged with victory. When you keep this thought in mind, it will make you realize that it is never, ever too late for you to dream. Joseph's dream was beginning to unfold when he was made in charge of his master's house. *And his master saw that the Lord was with him and that the Lord made all he did to prosper in his hand. So Joseph found favor in his sight, and served him. Then he made him overseer of his house, and all that he had he put under his authority. (Genesis 39:3-4)*

To increase our potential in the fulfillment of our dream, we need to overcome our insecurities about doing what God has entrusted us with. Joseph's master identified that his servant had a unique rapport with others. He recognized that Joseph was an intelligent young man with organizational skills, and for that reason he trusted him with his affairs. On the other hand, Joseph knew his limitations. He did not give in to the lustful nature of his master's wife, though she did all she could to have Joseph sleep with her.

What do we do when we are faced with difficulties in life? For example, you could apply for a job for which you are highly qualified, but the boss brushes off your merits. He then begins putting out vague hints about an improper relationship with you in exchange for your employment.

Here's another dilemma. You have applied for a major contract in business which you win, and you feel that God has answered your prayer at last. While you are about to settle in, you are introduced to what the 'business' is all about. You are to be involved in an unethical project. As a believer, would you give in and assume that God has answered your prayer? Or would you pull out and refuse to compromise, knowing that your God is more than enough?

Joseph did his best to believe God would make a way for him. Of course he faced ugly consequences for his loyalty to God. Yet he never cursed God in spite of receiving evil for good.

His third phase in the wilderness came when he paid dearly for his rejection to Potiphar's wife. In Genesis 39: 9-17 we read how she falsely accused Joseph of misconduct. Joseph was imprisoned as a result. He did not allow Potiphar's wealth to distract him, or his wife to compromise his faith.

"Then Joseph's master took him and put him into the prison, a place where the King's prisoners were confined. And he was there in the prison. But the Lord was with Joseph and showed him mercy, and He gave him favor in the sight of the keeper of the prison" (Genesis 39:20-21).

Joseph was a chosen man. God's divine protection was upon him. This brand of commitment is a rarity in our generation. Instead of standing firm in our faith towards God, we would rather give in to make it easier for us, compromising everything that God has entrusted to us. We would rather play popular tunes, and preach popular doctrines, knowing well that they are wrong, but we do it anyway just because it is what the crowd fancies. We prefer popularity and stack Christ's truth on the shelf.

While in prison Joseph had ministered to several men, and only asked that they would return the favor when they were released from prison. All he got from them were empty promises. They quickly forgot about Joseph when they left.

"Yet the chief butler did not remember Joseph, but forgot him" (Genesis 40:23).

At this stage in your life many might come to you for help because of the gift or position that God has instilled in you, but beware that some might express empty promises. It is imperative to use wisdom to know your boundaries. Remember such people are sometimes there to exploit you or even frustrate your destiny. Forget not about individuals such as Potiphar and Joseph's brothers who developed a terribly low opinion of the young man. When others look down on you and perhaps even slander you, keep reminding yourself that your reward comes from God, and when your time has come, no one can stop your blessings.

Pharaoh had a dream which no one could interpret. The butler recalled his encounter with Joseph. He confessed that he had committed a great fault by forgetting what Joseph did for him. Joseph was destined to be great, and nothing and nobody could stop him. God is faithful to those who trust and obey Him. Joseph's uncompromising nature gave him courage during hard times. God did not speak audibly to Joseph as He did to Moses. As we know, Joseph had a dream when he was young; he believed it and it came to pass. He knew he was different. He did not join in worship with the Egyptians, which would have been wrong, given the fact that Egypt had faith in other gods.

Many people have turned away from God, opting to consult psychics and new age beliefs for answers, yet their misery has not ended. They blame God when something negative takes place, even after believing in God for many years.

Nothing has changed over the past two thousand years. God is still in the same place He was when they crucified His Son. He too understands what pain feels like. Having a close relationship with God through Christ and studying the scriptures will give us hope in God's promises to us.

"When you pass through the waters, I will be with you; And through the rivers, they shall not overflow you. When you walk through the fire, you shall not be burned, Nor shall the flame scorch you." *(Isaiah 43:2)*

Was it wise for Joseph to have spoken about the dream to his brothers? No, humanly it was not wise. However, doing so did help to hasten his mission, though he was not aware of it at the time.

What would we do without our enemies? The enemy plots evil against us and God uses it for our good. Some negative situations are painful, and may seem like 'forever' experiences. For example, while in the hospital, I felt like I had been there too long, but I came out in God's perfect time. We have to pray that God will help us to grasp whatever He intends for us. We must not allow hatred to fester against those who have persecuted us. This will not only delay our breakthrough, but will prolong the emotional pain. God will not allow you to enter into your next assignment until He is sure that you have been transformed to what He wants you to be. Joseph never complained about his brothers. After he tested them to see if they had changed, he was happy to reveal to them that he was alive. His brothers were the ones who felt guilty for what they had done to him.

God is a businessman too! He will make sure you are qualified for His trust before you receive responsibility. One woman who came to the Lord with her need was tested:

"Then she came and worshiped Him, saying, 'Lord, help me!' But He answered and said, 'It is not good to take the children's bread and throw it to the little dogs.' And she said, 'Yes, Lord, yet even the little dogs eat the crumbs which fall from their masters' table.' Then Jesus answered and said to her, 'O woman, great is your faith! Let it be to you as you desire.' And her daughter was healed from that very hour" (Matthew 15:25-28).

Many of us would have failed had we been in her place. We would have felt insulted and turned our backs on the Lord. We pledge to volunteer in the work of God, hoping to get blessed, but we do not persist in claiming His power. We have created an ideal expectation of a minister of God, forgetting that we must humbly seek before we will receive the Spirit's anointing upon our ministry.

We wish to be placed in the category of 'celebrities' and we ignore those who do not belong in this category. It is becoming difficult for those in leadership in the body of Christ to lead a normal life. If the woman from Canaan was of our present generation *(Matthew 15:22-28)*, probably she would have ignored the Lord, judging him to be rude. Most likely, she would have left him with an unforgiving heart, going around telling people the young rabbi is not a man of God. She did not do that and, therefore, was blessed.

I had a dream and shared it with a woman whose reply was not encouraging. Her response was, "Do you mean you are going to go higher and leave us here?"

I was innocent and naïve. I did not know what would happen next. She then went away and shared my dream with her friends. They plotted against me. Their action ushered me to my next level of training.

I recalled that Matthew 5:44 says, *"But I say to you, love your enemies, bless those who curse you, do good to those who hate you, and pray for those who spitefully use you and persecute you."* Take courage in the Lord for He shall comfort you. Although it was painful at the time, I have forgiven and moved on. What happened was meant to usher me to my next assignment. In the case of Joseph as seen below his brothers deeply regretted their action.

"Then his brothers also went and fell down before his face, and they said, 'Behold, we are your servants.' Joseph said to them, 'Do not be afraid, for am I in the place of God? But as for you, you meant evil against me; but God meant it for good, in order to bring it about as it is this day, to save many people alive. Now therefore, do not be afraid; I will provide for you and your little ones.' And he comforted them and spoke kindly to them (Genesis 50:18-21).

Joseph's dream was fulfilled. Yet, he did not glory in that. Instead he reassured them that he was *not* God and was not to be worshiped. He made it clear that what had happened to him was only a manifestation of God's destiny for him.

God's plan for you is far beyond what you could ever imagine or expect. In due season, you will testify to the goodness of God. You will sing a love song to the Lord. It is unfortunate that we often get caught up in common events. We go around seeking sympathy from people rather than seeking the face of the Lord. God will redirect your path to the destiny that He has for you. Sometimes God sets up circumstances so we can hear from Him afresh. We need to be attentive and not miss His instructions. It is important to know to whom you are assigned so that you can receive counsel.

"Then the chief butler spoke to Pharaoh, saying: "I remember my faults this day" (Genesis 41:9). The vision is for the appointed time, and Joseph was now coming out of the wilderness. There had been no reason for the butler to mention Joseph's name to Pharaoh when he first came out of prison. God planned the right moment for Joseph to have a break-through.

He has ordained a perfect time to give you that miracle you so desperately need.

"Then Pharaoh sent and called Joseph, and they brought him quickly out of the dungeon; and he shaved, changed his clothing, and came to Pharaoh" (Genesis 41:14).

"Then Pharaoh said to Joseph: "Behold, in my dream I stood on the bank of the river. Suddenly seven cows came up out of the river,

fine looking and fat; and they fed in the meadow. Then behold, seven other cows came up after them, poor and very ugly and gaunt, such ugliness as I have never seen in all the land of Egypt" (Genesis 41:17 - 19).

Pharaoh sent for Joseph to interpret his dream. The grace of God gave Joseph a perfect interpretation. As a result, Joseph was appointed a governor of the nation. Finally, Joseph had reached his destiny. What a long journey!

You think your breakthrough is overdue? Joseph's took much longer; he lived with different families, survived being thrown in prison, and yet he never gave up. Spend time meditating on Joseph's experience and see the wonders of God in Joseph's circumstances. Our God is bigger and more powerful than all the troubles that come our way.

"And Pharaoh said to his servants, "Can we find such a one as this, a man in whom is the Spirit of God?" (Genesis 41:38). "You shall be over my house, and all my people shall be ruled according to your word; only in regard to the throne will I be greater than you" (Genesis 41:40).

Not only could Pharaoh identify the Spirit of God in Joseph, he also recognized the wisdom and revelation that God had given him. Even though they did not know or worship the Almighty, they confessed that Joseph was filled with the Spirit of God!

Chapter Five

Be Patient
Your Time Will Come

Joshua is a name of Hebrew origin, and its meaning is "Jehovah is salvation," Joshua was an attendant and helper to Moses during the Israelites' forty-year trek through the Sinai wilderness.

The Lord commanded Moses to lay hands on Joshua to impart the Spirit of God to him. *And the Lord said to Moses: "Take Joshua the son of Nun with you, a man in whom is the Spirit, and lay your hand on him" (Numbers 27:18).* One could imagine how the news spread among the Israelites, for Joshua now became the recipient of great respect. God often uses others to bear witness of His chosen person.

In later years, Joshua reflected powerfully the impartation that came upon him through Moses. This became evident when he commanded in the name of God the sun to stand still. The Bible says there has been no day like that, before or after that the Lord heeded the voice of a man, for the Lord fought for Israel (see Joshua 10:12-14).

In Joshua we learn that these feats became possible because Joshua allowed Moses to mentor him. (For a scriptural example of a protégé who never reached the destiny that God had for him, we will examine the life of

Gehazi in 2 Kings 5 later on). However, Joshua was of good character; he never whined, even when Moses rebuked him. Joshua was also extremely patient. He waited for Moses without complaint for forty days and nights while Moses received the Law from God on Sinai.

By allowing the Holy Spirit to guide us, we can receive wisdom to know how to respond in all circumstances. We should not forget that God, in His perfect time, will glorify Himself in our lives as we serve respectfully.

The Lord found Joshua fit to lead the children of Israel out of the wilderness. *"Joshua the son of Nun, who stands before you, he shall go in there. Encourage him, for he shall cause Israel to inherit it"* (Deuteronomy 1:38).

Christians often voice a desire to serve God, but they become confused by seeking the advice of too many voices. Others find a suitable way to serve God, but cannot accept instruction or correction. God is always fully aware of what we do with the talent He has given us *(see Matthew 25:14-30)*. Many talents are wasted because the owners are either not where God assigned them or they refuse to develop and grow in their assigned role.

As the Scripture states, we must study and implement the vision and call that God has for us. From the days of John the Baptist until now, the Kingdom of heaven suffers violence, and the violent take it by force (see Matthew 11:12). We must press on and refuse to give up. We should not forget the gathering of the brethren and the assembly of our local churches. How we behave in our places of assignment will determine our breakthrough from the giver to the receiver. In His perfect time, God will direct us to our breakthrough.

"But command Joshua, and encourage him and strengthen him; for he shall go over before this people, and he shall cause them to inherit the land which you will see" (Deuteronomy: 3:28).

Why would God trust someone with an assignment to lead His people if He had no confidence in the person's leadership ability? He knew Joshua was capable of leading the Israelites out of the wilderness because he had been mentored by Moses for many years. God told Joshua to march into the land despite its fierce inhabitants, and that He would allow the Israelites to inherit the land.

Wherever God places you, if you remain faithful, you will come through just fine. The hardship and trials that you go through should not discourage you. At one point, I faced a very difficult trial, and I began crying to God for help. As I was sleeping one night, I received a vision from the Lord showing a great army behind me. I believe God was reassuring me that I was not alone.

When Elisha was surrounded by the Syrian forces, his servant was terrified. *So Elisha answered, "Do not fear, for those who are with us are more than those who are with them" (2 Kings 6:16).* Similarly, Moses was confident that because divine forces went with Joshua, his successor was the perfect choice to lead. This was initially demonstrated by the peaceful transition as Moses passed the reins of leadership to Joshua. He even wrote a song on the same day praising God for Joshua. He inaugurated Joshua the son of Nun and said, *"Be strong and of good courage; for you shall bring the children of Israel into the land of which I swore to them, and I will be with you" (Deuteronomy 31:22-23).* Moses declared that Joshua would lead God's people to the Promised Land. He blessed him in the assignment ahead. Moses rejoiced, confident that the mission would be successful.

Joshua humbly listened to Moses. When we surrender ourselves to God, He takes away our insecurities, and His will becomes our will. Joshua did not have an arrogant, self-sufficient attitude like many of us do today. He led the people into battle and taught them the Law of God.

Current technology has allowed easy access to many leaders and teachers with varying beliefs and interpretations. One needs clear understanding to draw a line between these many teachings. Some have been led astray from the original message intended by God.

Christ, the only Son of God, became a servant and said if one wants to become great, he must first serve. Some Bible teachers tell people that we are sons of God and no longer servants, and that we should no longer be referred to as servants. Jesus Christ, the Son of the Almighty God became a servant and was not ashamed of it. We cannot separate servitude from son-ship with Jesus Christ the two go together, and one should be proud to be called a servant of God. Joshua became a great leader through serving, for he was a humble man. He obeyed Moses and followed his instructions without displaying a stubborn attitude or challenging his mentor.

Joshua was loved by the people. The wisdom he gained through his experience under Moses was invaluable. If we desire to achieve great things, we must work hard and sensibly. Knowledge in the Word will help us overcome every setback.

The scripture reveals that the Lord came down in a cloud and spoke to Moses. He took out of the Spirit that was upon Moses and imparted it to the seventy elders. Two men, Eldad and Medad, were not among those who went to the tent, yet they received the impartation and began to prophesy. A young man went to report them to Moses. Yet Moses was not threatened by the report; instead, he was pleased. A mature leader is pleased to hear good reports even regarding individuals he or she is not personally mentoring. Joshua was still maturing; he probably did not understand why those people were prophesying. He quickly asked Moses to stop them, and Moses rebuked him *(Numbers 11:25-30).* This had to be addressed so Joshua could learn how to delegate assignments, accept other's ideas, and allow people freedom to accomplish God's will in creative ways without his constant supervision or censure. For Joshua to become effective as a leader, he had to be taught how to integrate freedom into his leadership paradigm.

God told Moses that his time of death was nearing and commanded him to take Joshua to the tent to be commissioned. Moses did so and then presented him to the children of Israel. The Lord told Joshua to be strong and courageous for the assignment ahead.

It is normal to wonder how long it will take for us to reach our destiny. Once God reveals our destiny and mission, we again need courage to carry out the responsibilities that are expected. Joshua was commissioned to start the work of God in the presence of Eleazar the High Priest and the entire community *(Numbers 27:22-23)*.

When we are commissioned there may be no ceremony or pomp. What is important is that clear witness is given that God has called us specifically to a spiritual mission. Christ commissioned His disciples to take the Gospel forward to the utmost part of the world. Being commissioned is a way of witnessing to the body of Christ that we are ready for the work which God has entrusted to us.

Moses died at the age of 120 years. His eyes were not dim nor his natural vigor diminished, yet his destiny was accomplished and it was time for a new leader and a new phase in Hebrew history *(Deuteronomy 34: 1- 9)*.

After the death of Moses the servant of the Lord, it came to pass that the Lord spoke to Joshua the son of Nun, Moses' assistant, saying: "Moses My servant is dead. Now therefore, arise, go over this Jordan, you and all this people, to the land which I am giving to them-- the children of Israel" (Joshua 1:1-2).

Joshua had been referred to as Moses' assistant. By being with Moses he learned how to hear from God, which was imperative since God needed him to perform the work that Moses had left behind. He understood protocol. It is unfortunate we sometimes hear criticisms about other

70

ministers who have a team of protégées serving under them. What is a better way for these leaders to pass on the knowledge or the mantle? Christ had a team with Him which He sometimes classified in different groups. First he had a group of three, followed by a group of twelve and then the seventy as seen in the following scriptures:

Mark 5:37 -And He permitted no one to follow Him except Peter, James, and John the brother of James.

Mark 9:2 - Now after six days Jesus took Peter, James, and John, and led them up on a high mountain apart by themselves; and He was transfigured before them.

Matthew 10:2-7 - Now the names of the twelve apostles are these: first, Simon, who is called Peter, and Andrew his brother; James the son of Zebedee, and John his brother; Philip and Bartholomew; Thomas and Matthew the tax collector; James the son of Alphaeus, and Lebbaeus, whose surname was Thaddaeus; Simon the Cananite, and Judas Iscariot, who also betrayed Him. These twelve Jesus sent out and commanded them, saying: "Do not go into the way of the Gentiles, and do not enter a city of the Samaritans. But go rather to the lost sheep of the house of Israel. And as you go, preach, saying, 'The kingdom of heaven is at hand.

Luke 10:1 After these things the Lord appointed seventy others also,* and sent them two by two before His face into every city and place where He Himself was about to go.

Through the mentorship of Moses, Joshua became the greatest leader of his generation. Many have lost opportunities because they have under-estimated or belittled

71

the assignment that God gave to them. Joshua the young man who was assisting Moses in menial tasks became a great warrior. He led the people of God to the Promised Land. He had a conquering mind-set, and with the help from God he was able to lead victoriously. We, too, can achieve our mission successfully, but we must patiently wait on God to reveal it.

Chapter Six

Identify God's Purpose for You
Connect with People Committed to Your Success

"And Naomi said to her two daughters-in-law, 'Go, return each to her mother's house. The Lord deal kindly with you, as you have dealt with the dead and with me. The Lord grant that you may find rest, each in the house of her husband.' Then she kissed them, and they lifted up their voices and wept. And they said to her, 'Surely we will return with you to your people.' But Naomi said, 'Turn back, my daughters; why will you go with me? Are there still sons in my womb, that they may be your husbands? Turn back, my daughters, go - for I am too old to have a husband. If I should say I have hope, if I should have a husband tonight and should also bear sons, would you wait for them till they were grown? Would you restrain yourselves from having husbands? No, my daughters; for it grieves me very much for your sakes that the hand of the Lord has gone out against me!' Then they lifted up their voices and wept again; and Orpah kissed her mother-in-law, but Ruth clung to her. And she said, 'Look, your sister-in-law has gone back to her people and to her gods; return after your sister-in-law.' But Ruth said: 'Entreat me not to leave you, Or to turn back from following after you; For wherever you go, I will go; And wherever you lodge, I will lodge; Your people shall be my people, And your God, my God. Where you die, I will die, and there will I be buried. The Lord do so to me, and more also, if anything but death parts you and me.' When she saw that she was determined to go with her, she stopped speaking to her" (Ruth 1:8-18).

Ruth is a Hebrew name and its meaning is *friend* or *companion*. After the death of Naomi's husband and her two sons, she could no longer bear to stay in Moab. She preferred to go back to her homeland and asked her two daughters-in-law to return to their own families and remarry. They agreed, but then Ruth changed her mind, preferring to be with Naomi, while Orpah departed.

Ruth was a great woman, born with a purpose in the Kingdom of God. Following the events that took place later in her life, there was no doubt that her destiny was with Naomi. Although in the beginning her mother-in-law almost convinced the two to leave, Ruth was sensible enough to realize that Naomi had an important role in her life *(Ruth 1: 14).*

Ruth made up her mind that she would not worship idols, and instead she pledged herself to Naomi's God. As Christians, our behavior should be governed by the Bible. Our practices and lifestyles must align with the Word of God. Ruth knew that one cannot go back to the old life once the Truth is revealed. God honored Ruth as one of the great women in the genealogy of Jesus Christ. Her wilderness experience came through the painful loss of her first husband, brother-in-law, and father-in-law. Her refusal to let her mother-in-law go back to her people alone led them both into a place of blessing. The scripture recalls their arrival to Bethlehem was at the beginning of barley harvest in Ruth 1:22.

Ruth went through two phases in the wilderness. First

she married Naomi's son, which proved to be a link toward her final destiny.

Second, she worked in Boaz' fields. While there, she had no idea what God had in store for her. She thought she was merely working to earn a living for her mother-in-law and herself.

Naomi recalled that she had a kinsman of her husband's - a mighty man of wealth. His name was Boaz. At this point they were still saddened by the loss of their loved ones, but God had not forgotten them.

Sometimes when we go through pain we do not see any light at the end of the proverbial tunnel. Everything seems indescribably dark, and we wonder why God allowed us to enter this dark abyss. However, Ruth allowed her sorrow to draw her closer to God. Her mother-in-law was kind; her speech to her two daughters-in-law revealed a godly nature. Thus, Ruth realized there is a God more powerful than the ones she used to worship.

Ruth was able to recognize the hour of her destiny as it began to unfold. She was with the right people at the right place. She was submissive to her mentor, Naomi, who, by the grace of God, prepared her for the moment of her breakthrough *(Ruth 2:2)*.

Ruth was destined to marry Boaz. This would not have happened had she not married Naomi's son. Also, Ruth was a Moabitess. It would have been unlawful for a Moabite to be married to a Jew, yet God made a way. Her earlier marriage divinely prepared her for her destiny.

Ruth had positive qualities: she was humble, willing to learn, and quite industrious. Despite her lowly position in life, she did not become anxious because she believed God would sort their lives out for the better. Greatness and all that is associated with it requires us to be willing to learn. Nothing is free in life, let alone the anointing from God. For us to receive this anointing, God will test us to ensure that we can handle it. Serving other men and women of God is just one way of getting it. Even so, we must be governed by the Word of God, refusing to be discouraged by people or events and always remembering God's promises.

It might be that Ruth, apart from being discouraged by her mother-in-law not to stay there, had other issues. Despite those circumstances, she took the responsibility to make the right decision for her future. When we are selfless, God moves in to take care of us. Decisions we seem constrained to make in life sometimes may not make sense. In fact, they may cause those around us to think that we have lost our sanity.

It is important to be sure within us that this is the right thing to do. We must depend on the Holy Spirit and involve Him in every plan we make. He is attentive to us, and if we listen carefully we will hear His still voice deep within our hearts. Once we are convinced that we have heard from God through His Holy Spirit, then we need not worry. The Lord makes it clear that His sheep know His voice, and they must listen to none other. *(John 10: 27- 30)*.

Once we hear from God, we must refuse to be swayed by false doctrines or pessimistic people. No offense can stop us from reaching our destiny. Ruth refused to give in to negative events around her. She left the past behind and allowed the future to take its course.

When Christ's disciples heard His teaching that it is hard for a rich man to enter the Kingdom of heaven, they could not fully understand this concept, given the fact that God supposedly blesses His favored ones with wealth, and they themselves had abandoned almost everything in order to be with the Lord. The Lord reassured them that a hundredfold would be given to those who have left everything for His name's sake, both in this world and in the world to come *(Matthew 19:23-29)*.

Ruth left everything to follow her mother-in law, Naomi, into a foreign land, despite the older woman's many attempts to dissuade her. There was no guarantee of a good life for Ruth when she left Moab to follow Naomi, but she did so with a kind heart, believing Naomi needed someone to cater to her after losing her husband and two sons. This act of selflessness propelled her toward her destiny.

Likewise, Elijah tried to discourage Elisha from following him as his time for his departure neared. Elisha was quick to understand that the season for him to receive the mantle had come. He was not ready to allow any gossiper, miracle-chaser, or 'wanna-be' tamper with his future. He faithfully followed Elijah, and then the time came for him to receive his reward.

Some individuals have tried to encourage me to leave my God-ordained connection on different occasions. They speak cordially and say that I would be far better off by myself.

After we are anointed for service, we may have to wait for a long time without any significant positive harvest in our ministry, while newcomers may achieve their breakthrough much quicker. Because of this, other people may see our ministry as being outside of God's will. But should we leave if God has not said so? No! We should wait for God to direct us rather than going by the opinions of others. Even though, Elisha was matured, he waited for the appointed time for the mantled to be handed down to him. Boaz began to notice Ruth. His servant told him Ruth was the young Moabitess who had come back with Naomi from Moab. He went on to tell Boaz that Ruth had pleaded with him to allow her to gather after the reapers among the sheaves. Later Boaz spoke to Ruth and advised her not to glean in another field. He encouraged her to stay close by his young women and he warned the young men to leave her alone *(Ruth 2:6-10)*.

By serving Boaz, Ruth found favor and protection. She began to receive the reward for her commitment to Naomi. The Word of God tells us that we should not be weary of doing good, for in due time we shall reap a harvest if we do not give up *(See Gal. 6:9)*.

What will we do if calamity strikes those to whom we are assigned? Ruth did not run away from Naomi at her darkest hour.

78

Finding an exit during this time could cost you your destiny. At times, people do not place value on their work for God. They have no respect at all for their calling. They allow everything to become common and familiar, and familiarity can breed contempt.

When you pledge your service to God, you must understand that God is using your leadership as a channel to Him. You could lose the blessing if you take for granted those that God has placed under you or above you. The ministry will lack effectiveness because you deprive yourself of the input God's anointing would have made in you and through you.

It is possible to think of those above us as just people, forgetting that they are representing God. They are human beings with faults just like any of us, but we should not allow our ego to cause us miss God's blessings. Though we may be quite able and responsible, we need to accept the fact that our spiritual superiors are placed by God in a supervisory role. We must understand that God chooses to use them despite their weaknesses. It is possible for us to think we are serving mere humans, therefore respect does not matter, but it is not so with God. Your faithfulness and loyalty will determine your blessing. God has placed you there so He can impart the anointing on you. None of us can say who God should or should not use. Though Ruth lived with an aging mother-in law, she did not allow herself to look down on Naomi. She paid attention to Naomi's instructions.

Boaz received a good reference from people about Ruth. Clearly, people had been talking about Ruth's kindness toward her mother-in-law. They also noted that Ruth had left her family and her life to join Naomi in a foreign land *(Ruth 2: 11-12)*.

Boaz, being an elder in the clan, blessed Ruth for her kindness. He prayed that Ruth would receive a full reward from the Lord. Boaz did not know that he would come to play a role in Ruth's destiny.

"Then she said, 'Let me find favor in your sight, my lord; for you have comforted me, and have spoken kindly to your maidservant, though I am not like one of your maidservants'" (Ruth 2:13).

Ruth was a grateful woman; she noted that Boaz spoke kindly to her, though she was not one of his maidservants, and she thanked God. She faithfully continued to glean on Boaz's field waiting for God's ordained time for her breakthrough. We should not take it for granted when God rains his favor down on us.

Like Ruth, we also need to believe God for favor among men. Favor makes a way and can take you to places you never imagined possible. We need God's favor to overcome the trials the enemy throws at us. Prayer and intercession for the plan of God concerning your life must be offered without ceasing.

Honesty was another fine quality Ruth possessed. She was truthful with her mother-in law. She made sure that Naomi was aware of every detail that took place in the field. As a servant, loyalty is a requirement. Because of Ruth's transparency, Naomi was able to pray, guide, and bless Ruth.

This helped Naomi pray effectively. Our honesty to those whom we are assigned can cause us to receive unexpected blessings.

And her mother-in-law said to her, "Where have you gleaned today? And where did you work? Blessed be the one who took notice of you." So she told her mother-in-law with whom she had worked, and said, "The man's name with whom I worked today is Boaz." Then Naomi said to her daughter-in-law, "Blessed be he of the Lord, who has not forsaken His kindness to the living and the dead!" And Naomi said to her, "This man is a relation of ours, one of our close relatives." Ruth the Moabitess said, "He also said to me, 'You shall stay close by my young men until they have finished all my harvest. (Ruth 2:19-21).

"Then Naomi her mother-in-law said to her, 'My daughter, shall I not seek security for you that it may be well with you?'" (Ruth 3:1).

Because of Ruth's honesty Naomi became more positively involved in Ruth's life, and she wanted to make sure that Ruth was secure. This blessing would not have happened had Ruth clammed up or chosen to act selfishly. It is not good to hold back information, especially to a mentor. We should never forget that the Holy Spirit is watching and recording everything that we do.

It is important to observe who speaks into our lives and what they are saying. Words are powerful and can produce positive or negative consequences, depending on the person who releases them. Your mentor is an influential person in your life, and Ruth's example shows that we need

81

to take this seriously. God can use a mentor to straighten your path toward the assignment that He has for you. The training time should be taken seriously, and observations from your mentor are important.

Naomi coached Ruth to clean and dress herself becomingly before she went to Boaz' threshingfloor. She gave her attention to Ruth and told her what she should do when she reached Boaz. Ruth did exactly as Naomi instructed her. And it worked!

However sufficient we think ourselves to be, there are certain things God wants us to learn. It would be foolish to think that we are better than others---old enough or experienced enough to head straight into our ministry. Even though we may know some of the things necessary to perform tasks assigned by God, it is wise to allow ourselves to learn from others. You may be surprised that there are many ways to achieve the same goal and our way may not be the best or most efficient.

"Therefore wash yourself and anoint yourself, put on your best garment and go down to the threshing floor; but do not make yourself known to the man until he has finished eating and drinking. Then it shall be, when he lies down, that you shall notice the place where he lies; and you shall go in, uncover his feet, and lie down; and he will tell you what you should do." And she said to her, 'All that you say to me I will do.' So she went down to the threshing floor and did according to all that her mother-in-law instructed her. And after Boaz had eaten and drunk, and his heart was cheerful, he went to lie down at the end of the heap of grain; and she came softly, uncovered his feet, and lay down.

Now it happened at midnight that the man was startled, and turned himself; and there, a woman was lying at his feet" (Ruth 3:3-8).

Boaz was kind to her that night. After her visit to Boaz, Ruth told Naomi what had happened. Naomi was happy. She pronounced more blessings over Ruth and decreed that Boaz would not rest until he fulfilled his duty as kinsman redeemer.

"So when she came to her mother-in-law, she said, 'Is that you, my daughter?' Then she told her all that the man had done for her." Then she said, 'Sit still, my daughter, until you know how the matter will turn out; for the man will not rest until he has concluded the matter this day'" (Ruth 3:16 and 18).

Every true mentor of God is proud when seeing good fruits proceeding from those whom God has placed under their care. The true ones know who they are in God and are contented with the plan God has for them. We need to value and pray for them. Naomi was committed to seeing the fulfillment of God's plan in Ruth's life.

Here comes the reward! After having endured pain, the loss of her husband, and the long journey to a foreign land, Ruth qualified for God's blessing and reached the place where she could realize her destiny.

Most of us are unaware of the time frame between our preparation and the materialization of our destiny. I once watched a TV program where a woman testified that it took her sixteen years to reach the calling that God had for her. I personally received a vision from God in 1992, sixteen years later – 2008, I am just beginning to walk in it!

Ruth was rewarded publicly, nothing could stand in the way of her blessing. *So Boaz took Ruth and she became his wife; and when he went in to her, the Lord gave her conception, and she bore a son. Then the women said to Naomi, "Blessed be the Lord, who has not left you this day without a close relative; and may his name be famous in Israel! And may he be to you a restorer of life and a nourisher of your old age; for your daughter-in-law, who loves you, who is better to you than seven sons, has borne him." Ruth 4:13-15*

Just a few of the good qualities she possessed are faithfulness, loyalty, humility, honesty, and obedience. These qualified her to become one of the great women in the genealogy of Jesus Christ. God rewarded her!

The Lord will do the same for you if you follow His instructions and remain obedient to Him: *"Eye has not seen, Nor ear heard, nor have entered into the heart of man the things God has prepared for those who love Him"* (1 Corinthians 2:9).

Chapter Seven

Is Your House Built On the Rock?
Stay Focused by Keeping yourself Holy

Samuel is a Hebrew name; its meaning is "God heard" or "requested of God" *(1 Sam 1:20)*. Hannah, Samuel's mother was barren for many years. This did not make life easy for her, especially when Peninnah, the other co-wife, conceived children and mocked Hannah relentlessly. As part of their custom, they went to Shiloh yearly for worship and sacrifice to the Lord Almighty. That was where Hanna chose to ask God to grant her a son. She vowed to God that she would give the child to the Lord all the days of his life. She kept her vow after the birth of Samuel *(1 Sam 1:11, 1 Sam 1:24, and 1 Sam 2:11-21)*.

Dedicating your life and your longings to God will bring out the best in you. It does not matter how you look, what your income is, or whether you are young or old; God is ready to use anyone who wants to serve Him. Hannah's prayer was an enlightening breakthrough and encourages us to be specific when we pray. Through prayer we are able to change our misfortune. We can decide our future when we pray, as long as we keep our vows to the Lord. Hannah believed God for a male child and kept her vow to God.

Young Samuel's assignment was challenging. At the temple, Eli was being bullied by his own rebellious sons.

They polluted the sacrifices offered to God. But the Lord was with Samuel--- protection and wisdom were upon him. Samuel did not mingle with the evildoers, but continued to minister for the Lord. His mother's intercession before his birth helped to steer him in the right direction. She surrendered Samuel to God and believed that God would take care of him against all odds.

In some cases, God allows us to experience hardship now to gain wisdom enough to handle tough matters in the future.

"Now the sons of Eli were corrupt; they did not know the Lord. And the priests' custom with the people was that when any man offered a sacrifice, the priest's servant would come with a three-pronged flesh-hook in his hand while the meat was boiling. Then he would thrust it into the pan, or kettle, or cauldron, or pot; and the priest would take for himself all that the flesh-hook brought up. So they did in Shiloh to all the Israelites who came there. Also, before they burned the fat, the priest's servant would come and say to the man who sacrificed, 'Give meat for roasting to the priest, for he will not take boiled meat from you, but raw.' And if the man said to him, 'They should really burn the fat first; then you may take as much as your heart desires,' he would then answer him, 'No, but you must give it now; and if not, I will take it by force.' Therefore the sin of the young men was very great before the Lord, for men abhorred the offering of the Lord. But Samuel ministered before the Lord, even as a child, wearing a linen ephod" (1 Sam 2:12-18).

Eli's sons were a clear example that not everyone who calls God "Lord" will enter His Kingdom. Sad as it may seem, this is the reality. However, God's grace enabled

Samuel to serve the Lord with steadfast love, and he gained favor both with the Lord and with men *(1 Sam 2:26).*

While serving God we can either reap His blessing or His curse, depending on how we conduct ourselves. God wishes to bless us, but He has left us to make our own decisions.

Eli's sons received a curse from the Lord because of their behavior. (see 1 Samuel 3:14, 1 Samuel 4:10-11). On the other hand Samuel was being groomed for God's assignment as a future Prophet of Israel. *"Then the boy Samuel ministered to the Lord before Eli. And the word of the Lord was rare in those days; there was no widespread revelation" (I Samuel 3:1).*

The child Samuel was wise even at a tender age. He did not involve himself in the perversions of Eli's sons. He was obedient to God and to Eli. Samuel portrayed the importance for each one of us to channel our faith to God. A good example of the concept of adaptation to leadership is seen when Eli decided to mentor Samuel for his succession since his sons could no longer listen to him. Involving ourselves with disobedient people can cost us our destiny. Samuel kept himself pure, and as a result, he became one of the Major Prophets in biblical history.

Late one night the Lord called Samuel three times, but Samuel could not recognize His voice. He thought Eli had called him. During training, it is possible to miss God's voice because one is still learning. Eli taught the boy how to respond when he heard the same voice again.

Even Elijah, the great prophet, had to listen keenly to find out whether it was God's voice speaking to him! *"Then He said, 'Go out, and stand on the mountain before the Lord.' And behold, the Lord passed by, and a great and strong wind tore into the mountains and broke the rocks in pieces before the Lord, but the Lord was not in the wind; and after the wind an earthquake, but the Lord was not in the earthquake; and after the earthquake a fire, but the Lord was not in the fire; and after the fire a still small voice. So it was, when Elijah heard it, that he wrapped his face in his mantle and went out and stood in the entrance of the cave. Suddenly a voice came to him, and said, 'What are you doing here, Elijah?'"* (I Kings 19:11-13).

The Psalm below describes the awesomeness of God through varied expressions of His voice. It is important to understand the voice of God. Many people claim to hear God, though God is not even speaking to them.

"Give unto the Lord, O you mighty ones, Give unto the Lord glory and strength. Give unto the Lord the glory due to His name; Worship the Lord in the beauty of holiness. The voice of the Lord is over the waters; the God of glory thunders; the Lord is over many waters. The voice of the Lord is powerful; the voice of the Lord is full of majesty. The voice of the Lord breaks the cedars, yes, the Lord splinters the cedars of Lebanon. He makes them also skip like a calf--Lebanon and Sirion like a young wild ox. The voice of the Lord divides the flames of fire. The voice of the Lord shakes the wilderness; the Lord shakes the Wilderness of Kadesh. The voice of the Lord makes the deer give birth, and strips the forests bare; and in His temple everyone says, 'Glory!' The Lord sits enthroned at the Flood, and the Lord sits as King forever. The Lord will give strength to His people; the Lord will bless His people with peace" (Psalms 29).

The work of a mentor is to help the protégé stay on the right track with God. Samuel thought Eli was calling him. It would have taken him a long time to understand how to respond to God had Eli not taught him. A mentor becomes useful because of his or her expertise to move us forward. Wisdom comes through experience.

"Then I will raise up for Myself a faithful priest who shall do according to what is in My heart and in My mind. I will build him a sure house, and he shall walk before My anointed forever" (I Samuel 2:35). God declared that He would raise Himself up a faithful priest who would do according to His will. Are you one of them? God is always busy recruiting new servants; you could come out of the wilderness into God's marvelous light. His people in the wilderness are a people with a destiny! He is looking for people who are hungry to do His will.

Eli was a humble master who knew well that he had fallen out of God's favor because of his sons. But he was not jealous of Samuel; rather, he was glad to teach him. This shows his proven love toward God's work, and his commitment to the Kingdom of God. Eli was a good mentor to Samuel, though he could not bring the best out of his own children.

"Now the Lord came and stood and called as at other times, 'Samuel! Samuel!' And Samuel answered, 'Speak, for Your servant hears'" (I Samuel 3:10).

Although God may have called you, practical training from an experienced mentor is usually imperative. Samuel did well in listening to God's voice after receiving instruction from Eli. He heard every word from the Lord regarding Eli and his family. Samuel did not rush to deliver the message to Eli, though he could have. He was saddened by the message and felt compassion towards Eli.

"And he said, 'What is the word that the Lord spoke to you? Please do not hide it from me. God do so to you, and more also, if you hide anything from me of all the things that He said to you.' Then Samuel told him everything, and hid nothing from him. And he said, 'It is the Lord. Let Him do what seems good to Him'" (I Samuel 3:17-18).

Many years later, Samuel was instructed by God to anoint David as King of Israel, and, again, tenderhearted Samuel mourned---this time for the disobedient King Saul. God even had to gently rebuke Samuel as far as Saul was concerned: *'Now the Lord said to Samuel, 'How long will you mourn for Saul, seeing I have rejected him from reigning over Israel? Fill your horn with oil, and go; I am sending you to Jesse the Bethlehemite. For I have provided Myself a King among his sons'"* (1 Samuel 16:1).

An important learning session came for Samuel when God sent him to the house of Jesse to anoint the next King of Israel. When Jesse brought forward his favorite sons, David was not among them. In his own father's eyes, David was not a fit candidate to be anointed by Samuel. At first, Samuel judged by appearances and wished to anoint one of David's older brothers. However, he ended up heeding God's voice and anointed the right candidate. Eli's mentorship proved vital for Samuel when making a crucial decision which affected the destiny, not only of an individual, but of an entire nation *(1 Samuel 16:6-13)*.

Samuel would not have been able to serve God correctly had he been intimidated by Jesse or David's impressive brothers. Should we worry when we are questioned by those around us? Or should we use our own initiative to convince people that we are chosen by God? No, we must simply heed God's voice and relay it to others.

David was busy in the field looking after his father's sheep. He was not even aware that Samuel was at his home, and he had no idea God had sent the prophet to anoint him. David wasn't charging around trying to protect his own rights or interests. We need not concern ourselves with others who may be competing with us, rather we should commit ourselves to what God has called us to do. God will find the means to guard the blessings that He has in store for us. He kept Samuel from anointing the wrong person.

Throughout his time in the wilderness under Eli, Samuel had done his assignments. He did not rejoice over the judgment of God on Eli. Samuel was humble. He was not selfish, nor did he have the attitude of a person who wanted to take over from Eli. It took Eli's persistence to make Samuel deliver the Lord's message to him. Was this Samuel's period in the wilderness? Yes, indeed it was. Can you imagine him having to deal with Eli's sons who slept with women in the tabernacle and abused the sacred sacrifices? Samuel must have agonized when he saw them trashing God's altar and behaving immorally, and he may have even been tempted to do the same.

Though Samuel had the ability to hear from God, he still recognized Eli as his mentor. Samuel had wisdom, he lowered himself before Eli. His mentor had to teach him how to be obedient in delivering the Lord's message, whether positive or negative.

However high our calling, let's not forget those whom God has used to steer us toward success in our ministry. Eli taught Samuel not to allow emotion or opposition to interfere with the work of God.

"So Samuel grew, and the Lord was with him and let none of his words fall to the ground. And all Israel from Dan to Beersheba knew that Samuel had been established as a prophet of the Lord" (1 Samuel 3:19-20).

Thus, from a young age, Samuel stood as a servant to a great priest in Israel. Because of his obedience to the Lord, none of his words fell to the ground. He did the Lord proud by completing his assignments. May Samuel's revelation remind us as servants and mentors to put God first above our personal feelings. May the Lord make faithful servants out of us, in whom He can delight Himself as He did in Samuel.

Chapter Eight

Obedience is Imperative
Fellowship With God Provides Access to the Spiritual Realm

Elisha's name is of Hebrew origin; its meaning is "the Lord is my salvation." Elisha was a faithful attendant and successor to the prophet, Elijah. The Lord spoke to Elijah, the prophet, and ordered him to anoint Elisha as a prophet to succeed him. So Elijah went and found Elisha.

"So he departed from there, and found Elisha the son of Shaphat, who was plowing with twelve yoke of oxen before him, and he was with the twelfth. Then Elijah passed by him and threw his mantle on him" (1 Kings 19:19). The scripture goes on to tell us that Elisha stopped what he was doing and agreed to accept God's call. Elisha sets a good example of how to be an obedient servant.

When God calls us, we need not resist or wish to fulfill our own personal agenda first. Doing so could cause major negative consequences in our lives. The Almighty God must always have His way.

When God called me, I resisted, not knowing that He was calling me to serve Him. After escorting a friend to her home, I continued walking, deep in meditation. Thoughts echoed in my spirit, and I actually thought I was speaking to myself.

I said, "Oh, me! Working in the church day and night and praying for people all the time---definitely not my style." I was comfortable going to church every Sunday, and that was all I was prepared to do. At this time, I had a temporary job at an American institution, while at the same time attending college in Nairobi, Kenya. The director called me to her office and said they were considering giving me a job which would eventually result in a permanent post. I prayed and asked God what plan He had for my future and whether it was with that organization.

The Lord came to me in a night vision and said, "You ask me whether there is a future for you in that organization?"

"Yes, Lord," I replied.

"You are going to be a powerful woman," He said. "More powerful than your current boss."

I said, "Lord, how could this be? I am younger than she and possess no experience."

He stretched forth His hand, touched my lips, shut my mouth, and then touched my head. I felt my mind turning within me. He took a rod and handed it to me. Then His presence faded away. This was my first encounter with the Lord! What an experience! God is real! I did not know what He meant then; all I knew was that my future was not in that organization.

A few days later my boss called me into her office and told me the board of directors had met and decided that they were not able to keep me. Tears rolled down my cheeks. They were not tears of sadness or disappointment because I already knew that would happen. They were tears of joy! Besides, the Lord had said I would be more powerful than my own supervisor, so I was convinced God had another plan. Obviously, something good was on the way. Although I was not sure what awaited me, I was filled with peace and tranquility I could barely explain. It has taken years on a journey of discovery for me to find out what the Lord meant.

At times God calls people who are busy in their lives. They could be in business or, as in my case, pursuing a career. Elisha was at his farm. The scripture tells us that believers are ordained for a specific task before their creation: *"Before I formed you in the womb I knew you; before you were born I sanctified you; I ordained you a prophet to the nations" (Jeremiah 1:5)*. When these people are born they seem to lead ordinary lives. However, a time comes when everything changes. It is not easy to let go of what one has been doing, whether it is a career or something else.

Elisha was anointed for a greater assignment while he was busy working on the farm. Elisha decided to follow Elijah. At the same time he wanted to go bid farewell to his mother and father, which did not please Elijah. *"And he left the oxen and ran after Elijah, and said, 'Please let me kiss my father and my mother, and then I will follow you.' And he said to him, 'Go back again, for what have I done to you?'" (1 Kings 19:20)*.

95

In other words, Elijah was saying, "Are you truly fit to serve God? You cannot put your hand on the plough and turn back. Elisha would probably not have given Elijah total commitment had Elijah not warned him. From this point onward he came to understand that total commitment was required from him by Elijah. It seems evident that it is precisely for this reason that He kept the Levites for Himself. They lived in His temple to give Him undivided attention and to serve God's people.

It takes the wisdom and grace of God to know how to separate these issues. To grab our attention, God had to take some of us to a foreign land with no family members nearby. God does allow this sort of period to take place in our lives so He can gain our focus and commitment. There may also be painful experiences which cause a total dependence on God. Sometimes being too close to family or friends actually proves unconstructive for the individual concerned.

However, Elisha was a generous and kind man; he only wanted to show his love and respect for his parents and friends. He went back, took a yoke of oxen, slew them, boiled them, and made a feast for the people. He then arose and went after Elijah.

The Lord said those who have given up everything for His name will receive a hundredfold, both in this world and in the world to come. Because of Elisha's faithfulness in his service to God through the prophet Elijah, God rewarded him with a double portion of the anointing which was upon Elijah. Elisha stuck by his mentor everywhere Elijah went.

When the elder prophet was about to be taken to heaven by a whirlwind, he tried to discourage Elisha from following him. But Elisha was sharp in the spirit, and refused to go. Elisha told his mentor, "As the Lord lives and as my soul lives, I will not leave you."

The sons of the prophets came to Elisha to tell him the Lord was about to take his master away. That was not news to him. He was well aware of that, and he told them to hold their peace.

God is looking for a faithful remnant who will cling to their place of assignment no matter what it takes. It is important for servants to know that during this tough period the Lord is preparing new levels of responsibility for them. In Elisha's case, Elijah was ending his earthly ministry. It was a time for him to begin his ministry, but he wanted to do it the right way. If one is not careful, one may easily lose the "mantle of blessing."

"Then Elijah said to him, 'Elisha, stay here, please, for the Lord has sent me on to Jericho.' But he said, 'As the Lord lives, and as your soul lives, I will not leave you!' So they came to Jericho" (2 Kings 2:4).

Elijah tried to get rid of Elisha for the second time, but Elisha insisted that he would not let go. God tests us in many ways to find out whether we qualify to receive the mantle. Elijah used many challenges to see if Elisha would give up. Elijah kept leading Elisha through a sort of obstacle course, telling him that the Lord had asked him to visit various locations.

If we, today, face such a challenge, we may well become fed up with our mentor. Perhaps we would question whether the leader is hearing from God, accusing him of trumping up "busy work" just to occupy empty time slots.

Have you ever noticed that when we hear good news or receive an easy commission, we are more than ready to accept that it is from God. But when the news tells us what we do not want to hear, we begin to question whether the message is really from God.

The third time Elijah told Elisha to wait for him, he had been sent to Jordan, and Elisha still refused to give up.

"And fifty men of the sons of the prophets went and stood facing them at a distance, while the two of them stood by the Jordan" (2 Kings 2:7). The sons of the prophets were observant of every detail, yet remained aloof, not wanting to exceed their boundaries. They were close enough to witness what was happening, yet watched from afar.

Elijah took his mantle, wrapped it together, and smote the waters. The waters divided here and there, so the two went over on dry ground.

When a man or woman of God steps onto the platform to preach, we may witness the power of God in action through powerful preaching or other supernatural manifestation. The audience only see the finished product. A servant, however, is privileged to see the work going on behind the scenes.

When Elijah took his mantle and struck the River Jordan, Elisha saw the practical side of the anointing. Elijah asked Elisha what he should do for him before he be taken away. With spiritual wisdom, Elisha said he would like to have a double portion of the Spirit's anointing. He knew that anointing makes the difference. He could have asked for material things, but he knew that once he had the anointing he could achieve anything in his life. When he asked for a double portion, Elijah said to him, 'You have asked for a hard thing, nevertheless, if you see me go, then you would get it.'

In other words, if you remain faithful and don't leave prematurely, then you will receive the double portion. How many have left prematurely to start a ministry, and now find themselves struggling? Elisha stayed till the end *(2 Kings 2:9-15).*

Then it happened, as they continued on and talked, that suddenly a chariot of fire appeared with horses of fire, and separated the two of them; and Elijah went up by a whirlwind into heaven. And Elisha saw it, and he cried out, "My father, my father, the chariot of Israel and its horsemen!" So he saw him no more. And he took hold of his own clothes and tore them into two pieces. - 2 Kings 2:11-12

In this situation, Elisha demonstrated the great respect he had for his mentor. Elisha was not power-hungry; he was sad to see Elijah taken away. He must have wondered whether he was ready for the assignment ahead. He barely knew of his assignment, yet he was rewarded for being faithful to Elijah. Elisha called on the God of Elijah using

Elijah's mantle; as a result, the river, Jordan, parted and he was able to cross over.

The sons of the prophets gave witness that the Spirit of Elijah did indeed rest on Elisha. They came to meet him and bowed to the ground before him. Be encouraged; keep up the good service. God will bless you openly as he did for Elisha.

However, though the sons of the Prophets were all there to see God's blessing at work on Elisha, these young prophets thought they knew everything. They could not believe that Elijah had been taken by God. They urged Elisha saying, *'Look now, there are fifty strong men with your servants. Please let them go and search for your master, lest perhaps the Spirit of the Lord has taken him up and cast him upon some mountain or into some valley." And he said, 'You shall not send anyone.'"* (2 Kings 2:16)

But because they insisted so much, Elisha finally let them go. They searched for three days, but did not find Elijah. When they returned, Elisha said to them, 'Did I not say to you, 'Do not go?'" They did not believe Elisha when he told them there was no need to look for Elijah. They had to prove for themselves that something supernatural had taken place *(2 Kings 2:1-18)*.

The sons of the prophets could represent individuals who acknowledge that God can do unexplained wonders, yet attempt constantly to find other explanations for what He has done. They believe they are called to serve God, but refuse to trust God to move mountains. They have the

100

insight, but do not have the mantle. It is through service that the Lord releases impartation, and it takes understanding to admit it.

If one sought to find out how every mighty ministry called of God which we admire managed to get where they are today, one would find that the leaders started out serving in lowly positions, not just for one year, but for a number of years. They did not serve so they could develop large ministries, but, rather, they did it out of love for God. They never tried to curtail the years spent learning and growing. Though they are successful today, they have never stopped speaking well of those they served. It was not a smooth road, but they recognize the anointing of God must be respected. It does not matter what size of ministry the Lord has for us, the path to greatness in God's Kingdom is the same for all.

In serving God we are able to express our love to Him. God can do a wonderful work in each one of us. If we look deeply, we can see God in almost every step of our lives, starting from the time we get out of bed in the morning to the time we retire in the evening. We are blessed in ten thousand ways, and our service to God should be out of loyalty to Him, and for no other reason. The psalmist said that God is a discerner of hearts. He will distinguish the sheep from the goats. He knows those who are genuine and those who are not.

In a nursing career it is possible to distinguish between the one who took the job as a ministry and the one who took it as a means of convenience simply to pay the bills. These two individuals can be recognized by the way they relate to the patients. Similarly by loving God and all that pertains to His work, we are able to express His love to others. Christ made sure that Peter truly loved Him before asked him to feed His sheep.

So when they had eaten breakfast, Jesus said to Simon Peter, "Simon, son of Jonah, do you love Me more than these?" He said to Him, "Yes, Lord; You know that I love You." He said to him, "Feed My lambs." He said to him again a second time, "Simon, son of Jonah, do you love Me?" He said to Him, "Yes, Lord; You know that I love You." He said to him, "Tend My sheep." He said to him the third time, "Simon, son of Jonah, do you love Me?" Peter was grieved because He said to him the third time, "Do you love Me?" And he said to Him, "Lord, You know all things; You know that I love You." Jesus said to him, "Feed My sheep" (John 21:15-17).

The Lord asked Peter whether he loved Him. Is it not strange that Jesus would ask Peter this question after being together for years? The Lord mentored Peter for the ministry, yet he asked Peter such a question. We must recall that in Jesus' darkest hour, Peter had denied that he even knew Him. Now Jesus was testing him to see if Peter was someone he could count on to the very end.

Do we become involved in ministry because we want to offer our service to God, or because of what we can get out of it? Christ wanted to know whether Peter loved Him unconditionally and would serve him loyally. The Lord was not talking about physical food when He said to Peter "Feed My lambs; Tend My sheep." The Lord was charging Peter to teach His Word to His people for life.

There are many people today who are in bondage because of the lack of a proper knowledge of God's Word. The Lord said to Peter "Feed My sheep." Christ was confident that Peter had learned from his dark night of the soul and had received enough knowledge under His mentorship. Peter's denial of Christ was some form of wilderness. The agony he had to go through for those three days and nights must have been unbearable. Out of that he became a powerful man of God. Christ was confident that Perter gained enough experience to feed His sheep. He therefore wanted Peter to share it. Peter would not have qualified had he not been a servant first.

Let us return to Elisha's story. Evidently Elisha enjoyed being in Elijah's ministry. He was clearly sad to see Elijah go while Elijah,' on his part might not have been sad but contented in his mentorship of Elisha. Confident Elisha was ready to begin his own ministry.

Then the men of the city said to Elisha, "Please notice, the situation of this city is pleasant, as my lord sees; but the water is bad, and the ground barren." And he said, "Bring me a new bowl, and put salt in it." So they brought it to him. Then he went out to the source of the water, and cast in the salt there, and said, "Thus says the Lord: 'I have healed this water; from it there shall be no more death or barrenness.' "So the water remains healed to this day, according to the word of Elisha which he spoke. Then he went up from there to Bethel; and as he was going up the road, some youths came from the city and mocked him, and said to him, "Go up, you baldhead! Go up, you baldhead!" So he turned around and looked at them, and pronounced a curse on them in the name of the Lord. And two female bears came out of the woods and mauled forty-two of the youths. Then he went

103

from there to Mount Carmel, and from there he returned to Samaria."
(2 Kings 2:19-25).

Elisha became an important figure to his city. Suddenly, they noticed there was a problem with the water. They reported the matter to him. He prayed and the Bible reports that the water problem was permanently solved. The community was happy to enjoy good water. You can imagine how everyone began to testify that the God of Elijah was now with Elisha. He was referred to as the one who used to pour water on the hands of Elijah. Our training as servant-leaders is for our reference and to bring to account what God is *reaping* as a result of the period of spiritual *plowing* through which He prepared us.

Chapter Nine

Greed can Forfeit your Destiny
Bad Habits can Destroy Potential

The Hebrew meaning of Gehazi's name is not clear. He was an assistant to the prophet Elisha, but did not succeed him. This servant apparently failed his test and died in the wilderness. Gehazi did not reach his destiny because of greed and disobedience to the prophet of God.

"And Elisha returned to Gilgal, and there was a famine in the land. Now the sons of the prophets were sitting before him; and he said to his servant, "Put on the large pot, and boil stew for the sons of the prophets. "" (2 Kings 4:38).

Obviously, Gehazi exhibited some good qualities in the beginning. For example, when Elisha asked him to serve the sons of the prophets, he did not look at it as a lowly job. He served in all capacities; there was no job too small for him. To him 'it was a great thing to serve the Lord'. Another person would probably have wondered why he should cook for young men of his own age, yet he did not feel degraded by doing such menial tasks.

As a servant in the house of the Lord, we should not be choosy in the work assigned to us. Serving a man like Elisha who had a double portion of the anointing from Elijah, Gehazi may have been inclined to be spiritually conceited, but, evidently, he did not let pride stand in his way.

> *Then he said to Gehazi his servant, "Call this Shunammite woman." When he had called her, she stood before him. V14 So he said, "What then is to be done for her?" And Gehazi answered, "Actually, she has no son, and her husband is old." (2 Kings 4:12, 14).*

There is no clear hint how Gehazi came to serve Elisha. The scripture reveals that at one point Elisha had enough trust in him. This was demonstrated when Elisha sent him to the Shunammite woman to go and pray for her dead child. However, the Shunammite woman was reluctant to have Gehazi handle her case. This was an invaluable experience given to Gehazi by Elisha. Servants are sometimes not well received by those to whom they are sent to minister. Such people fail to understand that the person is under the mantle of his spiritual leader.

Gehazi was the one who told the prophet Elisha that the woman had no child. However, at this particular time she lacked the understanding that the anointing of God on Elisha could also rest on Gehazi. She refused to accept Gehazi as Elisha's right arm. Had she believed, Gehazi would have been able to bring her son back to life. But the Shunammite woman insisted that the prophet Elisha should go. It is no wonder Gehazi could not bring the baby back to life. As the saying goes, the anointing you respect is the anointing you attract.

It is possible that you have experienced rejection and even malice from the same people you are trying to help You spent time praying for them, yet they want you to fail in the task that God has for you.

Gehazi identified the woman's need, and this motivated the pronouncement of blessing from Elisha, who declared that the Shunammite woman would have a baby by the time he returned. By this time, Gehazi had been to all departments, cleaning, cooking and even on a mission to pray for the Shunammite woman's baby.

However, it is not how we begin but how we finish the race that shows our true character. Sadly, Gehazi became greedy. He could not understand why his master turned away the gift from Naaman. His lust for material things cost him his destiny. He betrayed his master, and brought a curse on his lineage. He used Elisha's name to take the gift from Naaman, and that was his downfall.

"But Gehazi, the servant of Elisha the man of God, said, "Look, my master has spared Naaman this Syrian, while not receiving from his hands what he brought; but as the Lord lives, I will run after him and take something from him." So Gehazi pursued Naaman. When Naaman saw him running after him, he got down from the chariot to meet him, and said, "Is all well?" And he said, "All is well. My master has sent me, saying, 'Indeed, just now two young men of the sons of the prophets have come to me from the mountains of Ephraim. Please give them a talent of silver and two changes of garments.' "So Naaman said, "Please, take two talents." And he urged him, and bound two talents of silver in two bags, with two changes of garments, and handed them to two of his servants; and they

carried them on ahead of him. When he came to the citadel, he took them from their hand, and stored them away in the house; then he let the men go, and they departed. Now he went in and stood before his master. Elisha said to him, "Where did you go, Gehazi?" And he said, "Your servant did not go anywhere." Then he said to him, "Did not my heart go with you when the man turned back from his chariot to meet you? Is it time to receive money and to receive clothing, olive groves and vineyards, sheep and oxen, male and female servants? Therefore the leprosy of Naaman shall cling to you and your descendants forever." And he went out from his presence leprous, as white as snow". (2 Kings 5: 20- 27).

In the Gospels, we read of a curious case in which Jesus cursed a fig tree because it was fruitless and, therefore, could not serve him: *"And seeing a fig tree by the road, He came to it and found nothing on it but leaves, and said to it, 'Let no fruit grow on you ever again'" Immediately the fig tree withered away" (Matthew 21:19).*

The fig tree promised fruit because that was, supposedly, its nature, but it was not true to its nature. We are living in the period of grace, and we hide under the blood of Jesus. Yet it is possible for us to become so consumed by lusts or greed that we lose all fruitfulness. We may even display a show of healthy green leaves, yet we are living a lie. An unsuccessful ministry or a church with stunted potential is just a few of the possible outcomes we bring upon ourselves.

And Gehazi, servant to Elisha, sold his soul for two talents of silver in two bags, with changes of garments *(2 Kings 5:21–27).*

Like his counter part Judas Iscariot may have begun well but had a bad end. Judas was one of the inner twelve Disciples. He had a vital role as a treasurer. Yet, in the end, he acted treacherously, betrayed his Master, and became the victim of suicide. He may have had great potential but he lost it just like Gehazi, unfortunately for a similar cause---greed and lust.

Matthew 26:14-16 tells us that Judas Iscariot received thirty pieces of silver to betray Christ: *Then one of the twelve, called Judas Iscariot, went to the chief priests and said, "What are you willing to give me if I deliver Him to you?" And they counted out to him thirty pieces of silver. So from that time he sought opportunity to betray Him."*

We need to pray that God gives us power to overcome greed. For instance, David was not over taken by self ambitions. He was anointed by God, and so was Saul. When Saul fell out of favor with God, David did not rejoice or see it as an opportunity for him to become the next king. He even had several ideal chances to kill Saul, but he did not. He understood that Saul was anointed by God to be king, and only God could remove him from the throne.

There may be Christian leaders we suspect of wrong. But we must keep our distance from those who speak against the anointed of God, lest we share in the curse from God on these people. We must make sure that we use the wisdom of God as our reference point. If we have proof that a Christian leader is enmeshed in serious sin, we may take a matured and respected Christian brother with us and approach this individual privately and humbly. However, we

109

must keep our distance from every slanderer, acting out a grudge, or speaking from hearsay. We must not allow ourselves to be used to destroy others' lives.

Elisha poured water on Elijah's hands and stuck with him no matter what; Joshua sat under Moses' tutelage and waited patiently for him for forty days and nights while Moses received instruction on Mount Sinai.

In our day Elisha might have been the equivalent of a chauffeur, driving Elijah to different events, yet he did not consider himself too great for such a thing. And we find no hint in scripture that Joshua ever complained against Moses of unfair treatment.

If a mentor does genuinely mistreat a protégé, we should remember God's word in *Psalms 135:14: "For the Lord will judge His people, And He will have compassion on His servants."* We should carefully pray for the persons involved and use scripture as a reference point to sort out the conflict. Otherwise, this can affect the person's relationship with God. Negative results from the experience can even put off the individual from serving God.

A lack of understanding sometimes results in brash, opinionated leaders who seek to lord it over their protégée and the congregation. They accept or reject individuals into various areas of ministry on a whim, or without knowing their gifts, or to discipline them for perceived weakness. These leaders refuse to acknowledge, we are one body with various functions and Christ is the Head. Some of us are assigned to serve under apostolic anointing; some are assigned under a prophetic mantle and others serve under a pastoral anointing one body---different functions *(Romans 12: 4-5)*.

If a leader is unwise or unruly, one must go through proper channels to either find another mentor or talk through the problems and find biblical resolution. In some cases, we must wait upon God for deliverance. God has ways in which only He can intervene in our circumstances. God's plan for us is that we should walk in love. Whatever one's function in the body, a servant's ultimate goal should always be to please God. With that kind of zeal God will eventually perfect everything that concerns the person.

Gehazi might have lived with sickness for a number of years after he parted with Elisha, but his ministry was no more. It ended before it had fully developed. The good works he did in the beginning are shadowed by the evil act he committed in the latter period. He could have been another of those individuals whom the Bible speaks of glowingly. Sadly, he did not make it. It grieves the soul to think of the lost ministry and what might have been had he stayed on the right path.

My prayer is that those of us left to do God's service will learn from Gehazi's mistakes and strive to never repeat them. May God help us.

Psalms 86:2 – Teach me Your way, O Lord; I will walk in Your truth; Unite my heart to fear Your name

Chapter Ten

Treasures can come from Unexpected Sources
Be Appreciative

The young servant girl at General Naaman's house became moved with compassion toward her master. In fact, we're going to see in this chapter how several individuals in that story combined forces to do good and heal this pagan, soon-to-be-converted, foreign general.

Most of us are touched when we see a suffering person, but we fail to take action. Images of suffering children from different parts of the world are seen on our television screens, as organizations appeal for donations. Yet there are many affluent people in the Western world who have never given a dime to help the disadvantaged.

A priest and a Levite walked past a man who'd been attacked by thieves on hi s way to Jericho. The Samaritan could not resist extending a helping hand to the wounded man. He cleaned up his wounds and boarded him at an inn and offered to take care of his expenses *(Luke 10:30-37).* How can we convert the world to Christ if we are selfish? The apostle Paul said we should abide in faith and hope, but the greatest of all, he said, is *love (1 Corinthians 13:13).* God is love, and we are created in His image. The godlier we become the more we want to extend Christian love towards others.

Back to the servant girl, she could not bear to see Naaman suffer. She believed that God could cure him. She said to her mistress, *Then she said to her mistress, "If only my master were with the prophet who is in Samaria! For he would heal him of his leprosy." (2 Kings 5:3).* Even though she was a lowly slave in a foreign land, the young girl wanted to help her master and mistress. Love appreciates everyone and likes to make people comfortable. Being kind to those whom God has brought our way may save us a great deal of heartache in life.

There have been stories in the media regarding some young women smuggled into the U.S. as modern day slaves. They were treated like animals, not allowed to go to school or to go anywhere alone.

One girl said she was not permitted to sleep on a bed like the rest of the family. She had to sleep on the floor. Thankfully, the government intervened and freed her. She was sent to college, having lost many years of education. Now her future is bright and hopeful, despite what she went through and she is not bitter and hateful toward her captors.

We do not have evidence that Naaman's Hebrew servant girl was abused, but she was certainly in a very undesirable situation. Everyone is someone's child and all are loved by someone. We need to come to the understanding that other people deserve the same treatment we want for ourselves. Naaman's servant listened and cared, and, for this reason, she was able to point Naaman to the only true and mighty God.

We need to be kind to strangers without being naïve or putting ourselves in danger: *"Beloved, you do faithfully whatever you do for the brethren and for strangers, who have borne witness of your love before the church. If you send them forward on their journey in a manner worthy of God, you will do well, because they went forth for His name's sake, taking nothing from the Gentiles. We therefore ought to receive such, that we may become fellow workers for the truth." (3 John 1:5).*

Naaman figured it was worth a try. However, when he tracked down Elisha, he found it detestable to follow the prophet's instruction that he should go bathe seven times in the River Jordan. In fact, he felt insulted because he could not understand why he should be asked to go wash himself, and why must he wash in the muddy Jordan when there were clear, crystal rivers in Syria. He had no patience at all, and almost packed up his stuff and hightailed it for home. If it were not for his aides, he would have done exactly that. *And his servants came near and spoke to him, and said, "My father, if the prophet had told you to do something great, would you not have done it? How much more then, when he says to you, 'Wash, and be clean'?" (2 Kings 5:13)*

Our behavior and treatment of others can affect our lives in either a positive or a negative way. Servants played major roles in Naaman's healing, from the housekeeper at home to his aide. They were, in effect, wiser than their master. The scripture stands true as indicated in *1 Corinthians 1:20: "Where is the wise? Where is the scribe? Where is the disputer of this age? Has not God made foolish the wisdom of this world?"*

Naaman thought himself to be intelligent. He mentioned the rivers in Damascus as superior to all the water in Israel. But he finally obeyed the instruction given to him by the prophet and, with the help of his aide, he was cured from leprosy. Later he proclaimed there is no God in all the earth except in Israel *(2 Kings 5:14-16)*. Having been delivered from the illness, Naaman could not stop praising the God of Israel. Prior to this time, he worshipped gods who had no power to cure him. Now, here was a tough-as-nails old pagan military leader admitting that the true God was the God of Israel! The young maid had gone from being a house servant to an evangelist.

The people in the story of Naaman were chosen by God to bring sense to this intelligent leader. We need to be humble in order to receive the blessings God has prepared for us. This way we will allow ourselves to go through the process that God has prepared to instill in us His wisdom. In the process, we may need to listen to those we sometimes consider below us in their ministry capacity.

Perhaps you are well-educated with a high profile background; how did you feel when God called you to work for Him? The process of brokenness can be one we resist strenuously. Some experiences tax your intelligence, and you tell yourself that you're losing your mind. You scream, "I have done everything right like I always do, so why is everything going wrong?" This is the doorway to the stage of brokenness. It happens to just about everyone who ever chooses to answer God's calling. This process is not your choice to make, nor is it respective of color, background, or

116

education. Unfortunately, it is an indispensable part of quality spiritual maturity.

Naaman lacked tolerance. He did not want to wash himself seven times, and was ready to quit before his God-ordained recovery. Many have given up because they thought their healing was too maddeningly difficult to bring to fruition.

Some may have been assigned to serve in trying places which God intended for a prescribed length of time, but they left before the mission was accomplished and their blessings could not be realized. They could not bear the pain of being broken. Some have been sucked in or distracted by the side whispers and gossipy opinions of how blatantly they are being used or abused. Eventually, they leave and forfeit what God intended for them.

In the beginning others are glad to do anything for the work of God. They try in every way to win favor from those under whom they serve, and by God's grace they earn respect. Then they begin to feel more important than others. Eventually, they come to despise fellow Christians whom they do not believe are their equals. Their ministry suffers, and gradually dissolves into nothingness. The outcome is never pleasant when we operate outside the plan of God for us.

The formula is simple; if there is no maturing process, there is no effectiveness. It is not a matter of choice for us. It is God's choice, and we can take it or leave it. God's laws of operative ministry never change for anyone. It is shocking to see how religiosity has distracted many from the plan of God. We need to submit ourselves to the mentors God has placed over us. Doing so will help us learn how to submit to God. Only then will God entrust us with the successful management of our own ministry. The mercy of God is upon anyone who is willing. The Samaritan woman was not Jew and was also an adulterous yet God had a plan for her life. Had it not been for Christ's coming she would have had no second chance in life.

The woman at the well in the Gospel of John commonly known as the Samaritan woman could not keep quiet after she had a meeting with Christ. While Christ rested at Jacob's well, this Samaritan woman came to fetch water. Christ asked her for a drink, and it amazed her that Jesus, being a Jew, would ask a Samaritan woman for a drink of water. In those days Jews had no dealings with Samaritans.

During the course of their conversation, the Lord asked her to go bring her husband. She said she had none. The Lord then told her that she, indeed, had spoken the truth because she had been married five times. He went on to say that the man she was with at that time was not even her husband. She said to Christ that she perceived him to be a prophet. She added: *"I know that Messiah is coming (who is called Christ). When He comes, He will tell us all things." Jesus said to her, "I who speak to you am He" (John 4:25-26).* Then the Lord ministered to her regarding the Living Water, and she immediately left, not even bothering to take her water pot, she went throughout the town telling people about Christ, and asking them to come meet a man who had told her all the things that she ever did *(John 4:27-30).*

God has a plan for everyone even those we consider sinful. I urge you to make a bold step and reach out to the rejected ones in the society. Christ made it clear to Peter, the person who had been forgiven most had shown much appreciation than the least sinner.

And Jesus answered and said to him, "Simon, I have something to say to you." So he said, "Teacher, say it." "There was a certain creditor who had two debtors. One owed five hundred denarii, and the other fifty. And when they had nothing with which to repay, he freely forgave them both. Tell Me, therefore, which of them will love him more?" Simon answered and said, "I suppose the one whom he forgave more." And He said to him, "You have rightly judged." Then He turned to the woman and said to Simon, "Do you see this woman? I entered your house; you gave Me no water for My feet, but she has washed My feet with her tears and wiped them with the hair of her head. You gave Me no kiss, but this woman has not ceased to kiss My feet since the time I came in. You did not anoint My head with oil, but this woman has anointed My feet with fragrant oil. Therefore I say to you, her sins, which are many, are forgiven, for she loved much. But to whom little is forgiven, the same loves little." (Luke 7:40-47)

It is hard to remain silent when one truly encounters the Lord. The woman at the well experienced liberty through Christ. She received understanding that Jews and Samaritans must worship the same God---not in Jerusalem or on the mountains at Samaria as before, but in spirit and in truth. Though she was a Samaritan, she expected the coming of Messiah. She expected the Messiah to reveal great truth to the world. No wonder she could not control herself after the Lord revealed Himself to her.

Since the beginning of creation, God's plan is for every soul to be in fellowship with Him. A multitude of people are still waiting to hear about Christ, who can bring redemption into their lives. The Samaritan woman had heard about a Messiah and was waiting for Him. People like this have a vague concept of God, though not in the right context; they are hoping they can somehow get to know who this God is. Such individuals as Naaman and the Samaritan woman have heard, but need someone to reveal the full truth to them.

"Jesus said, "I am the way, the truth, and the life. No one comes to the Father except through Me" (John 14:6).

The young maid and the Samaritan woman could not contain their excitement when they met the true God; they knew that others needed to know this Truth also.

Chapter Eleven

Rejection Cannot Ruin God's Forever Plan For You
You Are Not Forgotten

David was a remarkable personality. His name originates from Hebrew, and its meaning is "beloved." He was a shepherd, musician, poet, soldier, political leader, prophet, and king. After God rejected Saul, He instructed Samuel to go to Jesse's house where He had found Himself another servant amongst his sons, a man after God's heart, who pleased God with his worship. Jesse lined up his favorite sons, however, none of them were chosen by God. The brothers had the chance to waltz by the great prophet, each one hoping he had come to select him. Unfortunately, Samuel had not come to see any of them. Samuel asked Jesse whether he had any remaining sons. Jesse then recalled that David was in the field tending the sheep. Samuel asked he should be called. *(1 Samuel 16:1-12)* Jesse and David's brothers were all shocked that one of them was not chosen. They all had to wait for David to be called in from the field.

They were bewildered the runt of the bunch could be the one, but the choice was God's and His will is always good, pleasing, and perfect. God planned it so that David would stand out amongst his brothers. David would have behaved differently when Samuel went to anoint him, had he known the difficulties he was to face. King Saul chasing him with murderous intent was one such trouble obstructing his destiny. *(1 Samuel 19:1).* Nevertheless, what God had for David, no one could take away.

The Bible tells us David was ruddy, with bright eyes, and a handsome appearance. *"So he sent and brought him in. Now he was ruddy, with bright eyes, and good-looking. And the Lord said, "Arise, anoint him; for this is the one!" Then Samuel took the horn of oil and anointed him in the midst of his brothers; and the Spirit of the Lord came upon David from that day forward. So Samuel arose and went to Ramah." (1 Samuel 16:12-13).*

David's foot steps were beginning to be ordered by God so he could reach his destiny. His father sent him to the battlefield to deliver food to his brothers and requested him to report the progress of the battle. While there, David overhead a conversation between soldiers about Goliath defying Israel. He asked what reward would be given to the man who would defeat Goliath.

David might have been shocked when he overheard the soldiers discussing Goliath, the Philistine, with bravado; none of them even considered facing him. They perhaps thought David was a young upstart whom they could impress. Unbeknownst to them, his destiny was beginning to unfold. He ignored those who were putting him down, including his own brother.

You see, Eliab had heard his conversation with the men, and he became angry with his kid brother: "Why did you come down here? Moreover, with whom have you left those few sheep in the wilderness? I know your pride and the insolence of your heart, for you have come down to see the battle."

Eliab underrated David. He referred to the sheep as those 'few sheep' (1 Samuel 17:28). Eliab thought he was better than David; he was more of a man than his younger brother because he was on the frontline of battle while David spent his days in the wilderness with a gaggle of sheep.

Sometimes people think better of themselves than others do. The fact that one holds an important role or has achieved something important should not cause him to undervalue others.

David did not waste his time arguing with Eliab. He concentrated on important matters. He asked his brother whether there was cause for him to be so incensed. David realized that some of the obstacles he had overcome while in the field had become testimonies to position him for the battle ahead. David's inquiry about the war was relayed to King Saul, and he sent for David. The King told David that Goliath was an experienced man who had been in war since his youth. Saul considered David as a young man with no experience who thought he could fight Goliath.

Then David said to Saul, "Let no man's heart fail because of him; your servant will go and fight with this Philistine." And Saul said to David, "You are not able to go against this Philistine to fight with him; for you are a youth, and he a man of war from his youth." But David said to Saul, "Your servant used to keep his father's sheep, and when a lion or a bear came and took a lamb out of the flock, I went out after it and struck it, and delivered the lamb from its mouth; and when it arose against me, I caught it by its beard, and struck and killed it. Your servant has killed both lion and bear; and this uncircumcised Philistine will be like one of them, seeing he has defied the armies of the living God." Moreover David said, "The Lord, who delivered me from the paw of the lion and from the paw of the bear, He will deliver me from the hand of this Philistine." And Saul said to David, "Go, and the Lord be with you!" So Saul clothed David with his armor, and he put a bronze helmet on his head; he also clothed him with a coat of mail. David fastened his sword to his armor and tried to walk, for he had not tested them. And David said to Saul, "I cannot walk with these, for I have not tested them." So David took them off" (1 Samuel 17: 32-39).

According to the scripture, David did not give up. He convinced Saul that he was qualified to go fight Goliath. He detailed his experience in the wilderness and added to it that God was with him. We need to draw strength from God in every experience through which He takes us. Most importantly, we must not forget that we do not achieve victory through our own intelligence, but rather through God's power within us. David did not allow Goliath's size or wartime experience intimidates him, and he remained confident that God was with him.

For Christians the victory has already been achieved at Calvary where Christ declared, "It is finished." He was buried and rose from the dead on the third day. The Lord won the battle over every obstacle that comes our way. "All things are possible to him who believes." *(Mark 9:23).*

David saw himself as a victorious man before he even stepped onto the battlefield. It may have seemed as though

David was just a harmless shepherd, but as he defended his sheep, he learned how to fight victoriously.

It is surprising to note how many people underestimate their God-given talent. Some even think they cannot do significant exploits because of their age, their lowly family background, or their lack of education. The person you are looking down on today could be the one whom God will be using tomorrow.

Intimacy with the Holy Spirit will empower us with confidence to lead the life that God requires of us. In doing so we will develop wisdom to judge by the Word of God and not by what others think or say of us.

It did not matter to David what anyone thought of him because he knew who he was in God. He said to Goliath, "You come to me with a sword, with a spear, and with a javelin. But I come to you in the name of the Lord of hosts." He knew he could emerge victorious in any battle, so long as he had faith in God. The psalmist wrote, *"A thousand may fall at your side, and ten thousand at your right hand; but it shall not come near you. Only with your eyes shall you look, and see the reward of the wicked."* (Psalms 91:7-8).

We need not be shaken by the mountains blocking our way. If God be for us, who can be against us? From killing a lion to defeating Goliath, David won many battles while on his way to the throne. Having faith in God will always empower us to overcome the traps and the snares of the opposition.

"Then David said to the Philistine, 'You come to me with a sword, with a spear, and with a javelin, but I come to you in the name of the LORD of hosts, the God of the armies of Israel, whom you have defied'" (1 Sam 17:45). Therefore, it happened that David fought and killed Goliath with a sling.

Occasionally, one's destiny may be determined by the assignment. David was to be the next king, so there was no better place for him to be than among the king's men. His experience in the wilderness as a shepherd prepared him to be a skilled warrior, which later would prove useful on the battlefield. As a result, he was able to win many battles for his nation. His military exploits and skill in playing the harp won him favor before the king and he was promoted to live in the kingly quarters, now divinely positioned to gain exposure for his destined assignment as the future king.

David may not have been aware of it at the time, but God was unveiling his plan for him. He became an armor bearer to King Saul. This was to help him understand his future role as King of Israel, though he likely considered himself a common servant to the King.

Now it had happened as they were coming home, when David was returning from the slaughter of the Philistine, that the women had come out of all the cities of Israel, singing and dancing, to meet King Saul, with tambourines, with joy, and with musical instruments. So the women sang as they danced, and said: "Saul has slain his thousands, And David his ten thousands." Then Saul was very angry, and the saying displeased him; and he said, "They have ascribed to David ten thousands, and to me they have ascribed only thousands. Now what more can he have but the Kingdom?" (1 Samuel 18:6-8).

The Bible says that Saul eyed David from that day forward. Saul probably wondered what next David was capable of, after having defeated Goliath.

> *So Saul eyed David from that day forward. And it happened on the next day that the distressing spirit from God came upon Saul, and he prophesied inside the house. So David played music with his hand, as at other times; but there was a spear in Saul's hand. And Saul cast the spear, for he said, "I will pin David to the wall!" But David escaped his presence twice Now Saul was afraid of David, because the Lord was with him, but had departed from Saul. Therefore Saul removed him from his presence, and made him his captain over a thousand; and he went out and came in before the people. And David behaved wisely in all his ways, and the Lord was with him. Therefore, when Saul saw that he behaved very wisely, he was afraid of him. But all Israel and Judah loved David, because he went out and came in before them. (1 Samuel 18:9-16).*

Some things are best left alone without wasting time trying to figure them out. Let the future unveil itself. God mapped the plan to make David the next king of Israel, but young David could not see it then. Saul realized more and more that God's favor was with David, and an evil spirit of rage and jealousy began to torment him. The scripture details that 'the Spirit of the Lord departed from Saul, and a distressing spirit from the Lord troubled him.' His servants suggested that he should seek a skillful person to play music to ease his stress. The best candidate for the job turned out to be David. They gave evidence to Saul about David's qualities, and why he should be the one to play the harp for him as follows: "Look, I have seen a son of Jesse, the Bethlehemite, who is skillful in playing, a mighty man of valor; a man of war, prudent in speech, and a handsome person; and the Lord is with him." *(1 Samuel 16:18)*

Above all, they mentioned the Lord was with David. They distinguished that of all the good qualities David had, God was with him. This was important to help ease the evil spirit from Saul. *(See 1 Samuel 16:14-23).*

Tough times were just beginning for David when Saul sent for him at his father's house. It is written that whenever the evil spirit was troubling Saul, David would take a harp and play it with his hand. Then Saul would become refreshed and peaceful, and the distressing spirit would leave him.

David began his next level in the wilderness. Playing for Saul challenged him, but he soon discovered his life was in jeopardy. Saul had become so jealous of God's favor on David that he wanted to kill him. Saul knew how important it was to have God on one's side. During this time, David did not try to harm Saul; he waited patiently for the Lord to work it out. He respected Saul, knowing that he was anointed of God.

Your obedience will qualify you for your next assignment. Although Saul was distressed, God's plan for David was to familiarize himself with leadership. David faced horrifying encounters during the time he played harp for Saul. There were several attempts on his life when Saul threw a spear towards him.

After attempts to kill David failed, Saul could not handle him anymore, so he decided to promote David to lead a battalion. From a harp player to a commander in the army! Saul removed him from his presence and made him his captain over a thousand, and David went out and came in before the people.

This was a potentially catastrophic season for David. It was noted that he behaved wisely, which caused Saul to fear him even more. Saul hoped that David would get killed in battle with the Philistines. He asked David to be valiant for him and fight the Lord's battle. In return, he offered David his daughter, Merab, for a wife. David was not fooled by this, and when the time came for Merab to be given to David, she was given to someone else instead. Later Saul heard that his other daughter Michal was falling in love with David. Saul decided to give her to David so she would be a snare to him. (She was the one who later jeered at David when he danced before the Lord).

Saul's wish for David's death never came true, for God was with him. King Saul became obsessed to the extent that he began to chase David throughout the wilderness so he could kill him. David escaped every time.

One night David found Saul asleep. He could have killed Saul if he had so desired, but, instead, he took Saul's spear and the jug of water that were by Saul's side. He got away, and no man saw it or awoke. They were all asleep because a deep sleep from the Lord had fallen upon them. David told the servant who was looking after Saul that he had reneged in his assignment because he had failed to look after his master, Saul, the Lord's anointed. He revealed to him that he had come upon them and had taken the King's spear and the jug of water.

When God's favor is with a man, his enemies will not succeed in their schemes because of God's protective hand. When Saul heard why David had done what he did, he repented and asked David to return, promising not to harm him anymore. David asked Saul to send one of his young men to come and collect the spear and the jug of water.

"Then Saul said, "I have sinned. Return, my son David. For I will harm you no more, because my life was precious in your eyes this day. Indeed I have played the fool and erred exceedingly." And David answered and said, "Here is the King's spear. Let one of the young men come over and get it. May the Lord repay every man for his righteousness and his faithfulness; for the Lord delivered you into my hand today, but I would not stretch out my hand against the Lord's anointed. And indeed, as your life was valued much this day in my eyes, so let my life be valued much in the eyes of the Lord, and let Him deliver me out of all tribulation." Then Saul said to David, "May you be blessed, my son David! You shall both do great things and also still prevail." So David went on his way, and Saul returned to his place." (1 Samuel 26:21-25).

David knew how treacherous Saul could be, so, though Saul repented, David did not trust him. As a servant in the wilderness and a person with destiny, David understood the need to let God take control. He reasoned that Saul was a King anointed by God. Though Saul took every opportunity to have, David killed, and although David was aware of Saul's evil intentions toward him, he did nothing to fight back. In the end, it became clear to Saul that there was little he could do to stop David from being the King of Israel, but he tried to kill him to the end. May God help us all to understand the need to trust fully in Him, as did David, without fear of our enemies.

David was not only a skilled warrior; he gave his heart to God through worship. He was a humble man before the Lord, and he knew he could never hide from God, yet he was confident of the presence of the Lord *(Psalms 139)*. On several occasions, he committed gross sins, and he paid dearly for them. One such consequence included the loss of his infant child.

"Then David returned to bless his household. And Michal the daughter of Saul came out to meet David, and said, 'How glorious was the King of Israel today, uncovering himself today in the eyes of the maids of his servants, as one of the base fellows shamelessly uncovers himself!' So David said to Michal, 'It was before the Lord, who chose me instead of your father and all his house, to appoint me ruler over the people of the Lord, over Israel. Therefore I will play music before the Lord. And I will be even more undignified than this, and will be humble in my own sight. But as for the maidservants of whom you have spoken, by them I will be held in honor.' Therefore Michal the daughter of Saul had no children to the day of her death" (2 Samuel 6: 20-23).

David knew how to repent and get right with God, and he opened his heart to God with faith like a child. This becomes obvious to us when we see him dancing before the Lord as the Ark of the Covenant was brought back. David did not care about his surroundings, nor did he care for man's approval when it came to worshipping and pleasing God. The scripture details that David and the house of Israel brought up the ark of the Lord with shouting and with the sound of the trumpet. He danced before the Lord with great joy, appreciating what God had done for him. This disgusted his dignified wife, Michal, Saul's daughter. Her negative comments did not bother David, but they cost her. She did not have any children. Michal had no heir to the throne because she scoffed and jeered against the man of God.

You may not understand God's plan for you at this point, but that should not disturb you. David went from being a shepherd in the wilderness to one of the most powerful Kings in the then-known world. Yet, when God initially sent Samuel to anoint him, his own father, and brothers did not even consider him worth a glance. It took the Spirit of the Lord to prompt Samuel to ask whether Jesse had another son who might not be in their midst. David went from negative rejection by his brothers to victory over the monstrous Philistine.

Pay no attention to vision-killers. Follow your instinct and let the Holy Spirit guide you. Most people want to have loyal servants in ministry or churches, but only God can make that happen. All prayers and desires should be offered to God, believing that He will perfect everything according to His will. When we feel low, we should quote the promises of God, and read them often to renew our minds.

David was not only a King; he was also a man who loved God. The victories he earned in the war did not stop him from worshipping his God. He could not contain himself, and he was not ashamed of that.

We could all learn from this recurring biblical theme. Doing God's will results in blessings; complaining yields curses. We must shut out all the negative people with their mean-spirited jargon. The work of God must be done and can be achieved only by the faithful. I do not deny that we often come across problems---whether financial problems, relational conflicts, sickness, or the death of a loved one, but God is faithful to see us through. He can renew our strength every moment. I think of my late mother every day, every minute, but God has replaced my pain with hope. I have faith that she is with the Lord. She received Christ and was right with God before she departed.

Throughout David's time on the throne, he experienced both pain and joy, both problems and victories, losses and gains, yet none of these made him stop worshipping. He drew himself closer and closer to God to the very end.

Psalms 86:2 – Preserve my life, for I am holy; You are my God; Save Your servant who trusts in You.

Chapter Twelve

Don't Grow Weary in Doing Good
Your Labor Of Love Will Speak For You

"At Joppa there was a certain disciple named Tabitha, which is translated Dorcas. This woman was full of good works and charitable deeds which she did. But it happened in those days that she became sick and died. When they had washed her, they laid her in an upper room. And since Lydda was near Joppa, and the disciples had heard that Peter was there, they sent two men to him, imploring him not to delay in coming to them. Then Peter arose and went with them. When he had come, they brought him to the upper room. And all the widows stood by him weeping, showing the tunics and garments which Dorcas had made while she was with them. But Peter put them all out, and knelt down and prayed. And turning to the body he said, "Tabitha, arise." And she opened her eyes, and when she saw Peter she sat up. Then he gave her his hand and lifted her up; and when he had called the saints and widows, he presented her alive. And it became known throughout all Joppa, and many believed on the Lord. So it was that he stayed many days in Joppa with Simon, a tanner" (Acts 9:36-43).

Dorcas, also known as Tabitha (*Dorcas* means a *gazelle* in Greek; *Tabitha* is the equivalent in Hebrew), was a disciple of the Lord Jesus Christ. This woman was well known and loved because of her charitable work in the community. Many were inspired by her benevolent labors and wished to reach her standard. She lived in Joppa and appeared to be from a good background. She died after an illness, and this

135

left the grief-stricken community wondering how they would survive without her. They washed her body and laid her in an upper room.

Upon hearing that the apostle Peter was in Lydda, the disciples there sent two messengers to Peter, imploring him not to delay in coming to them. They testified that Dorcas had been good and generous toward them. Upon Peter's arrival, all the widows stood by him weeping, showing the clothes that Dorcas had made for them.

Never become weary of doing good; the Bible says we will reap if we faint not. Your goodness today will bear witness for you tomorrow. Dorcas came back to life because of the widows' intercession. They had a memory of her work, and could not imagine being without her.

It is rare to find a kind sweet nature like Dorcas'. This lovely woman was assigned to her community to provide for the needs of the poor. Clearly, not all of us can be preachers; some are assigned to the widows' ministry, and some to the orphans' ministry. Other people are working hard, making impact in the lives of many. Most of these people are involved in the background, and we are not even aware of the powerful impact they have made. Some of these people will never be publicly recognized, yet God knows them all. Before a revival can take place in a city or nation, an amazing amount of groundwork goes into it. Hundreds of believers exercise major intercession.

There are many people in the church today who are gifted to even initiate ministries, but they do not possess the means. Such people, if given a chance, could better the lives of many in society. We should seek to sponsor the worthy projects of such people, as long as what they are doing is genuinely for the welfare of people. One does not need to be rich to be generous. This is demonstrated through our offerings, which differ from one person to the next based on one's income. Volunteering our time to help in whatever way we can is also an offering. We need to find ways we can express Christ's compassion without compromising our faith.

One day I had such a migraine that it even hurt to brush my hair. I stopped by a shop that afternoon, and a woman gave me a spiteful glance and said to her friend, "Oh, sister, this weather is making it difficult to manage my hair."

I knew she was passing an indirect message to me about my unkempt hair. Given the fact she is a Christian sister, she could have spoken to me directly. Then she would have learned of my migraine and could have prayed for its relief. I left the place feeling discouraged.

While at a certain mission, a sister in the Lord was not using good hygiene. People gossiped about her body odor, but no one would speak to her directly. It became too much, and one day I went to her privately. Gently and tactfully, I spoke to her about the importance of cleanliness. She thanked me.

You may consider this a strange way to serve others, but we never know how we will be called upon to serve from one day to the next.

Your good works, despite discouragements, could bear witness at a crucial time. This was how it was with Dorcas' vital service to the widows. Her helpfulness toward others in her life caused these women to yearn that she would have some additional years of service on earth.

The Bible instructs: *"To godliness, brotherly kindness, and to brotherly kindness, love" (2 Peter 1:7).* During church services when we are told to greet one another, people cross from one side of the hall to the other to greet those with whom they are familiar, but, in many cases, they leave newcomers standing alone and feeling awkward. I have watched them when they come across newcomers; they fake a smile and utter an unintelligible greeting, not even bothering to look at them. They seem to be just fulfilling formalities. I sometimes wonder why they even bother if they do not mean it. The newcomer can easily tell from their expression that they are not genuine. How can we relate to people what Christianity is all about if we only care for those that we know and love?

The Lord said, "And if a house is divided against itself, that house cannot stand" (Mark 3:25). Lack of proper teaching and understanding has resulted in immature Christians being swayed by false doctrines. It is crucial to ensure the care and nurture of new souls by introducing them to good churches where the Word of God is soundly taught. Salvation without proper foundation will not result in mature, Christ-honoring believers.

One example of our poor follow up is seen in how few people are baptized after receiving Christ. The scripture states clearly that after repentance, one needs to be baptized. In Acts 2:38, it reads, *"Then Peter said to them, "Repent, and let every one of you be baptized in the name of Jesus Christ for the remission of sins; and you shall receive the gift of the Holy Spirit."*

Another problem in our churches is our rough handling of personal relationships. Some new attendees change their place of worship every time they feel offended. Lack of proper apostolic order has produced ungoverned authorities, and this has contributed to much distrust in the so-called churches. Yet if people are well grounded in the Word, they will understand the need to stay in covenant with one another as servants with mentors and as fellow saints with their church family.

When Dorcas passed, the people sent for Peter, their apostolic authority. He was asked to come help them to pray. Dorcas' work was recognized among the members in the body of Christ and Peter learned of it in detail. The testing period in her life helped expand the ministry. Peter stayed longer in the town because the multitudes were encouraged by her testimony.

Psalms 84; 9 – O God, behold our shield, And look upon the face of Your anointed.

Chapter Thirteen

There Is Power in Submission
One will be Like a Thousand

"Now in those days, when the number of the disciples was multiplying, there arose a complaint against the Hebrews by the Hellenists, because their widows were neglected in the daily distribution. Then the twelve summoned the multitude of the disciples and said, 'It is not desirable that we should leave the word of God and serve tables. Therefore, brethren, seek out from among you seven men of good reputation, full of the Holy Spirit and wisdom, whom we may appoint over this business; but we will give ourselves continually to prayer and to the ministry of the word.' And the saying pleased the whole multitude. And they chose Stephen, a man full of faith and the Holy Spirit, and Philip, Prochorus, Nicanor, Timon, Parmenas, and Nicolas, a proselyte from Antioch, whom they set before the apostles; and when they had prayed, they laid hands on them. Then the word of God spread, and the number of the disciples multiplied greatly in Jerusalem, and a great many of the priests were obedient to the faith" (Acts 6:1-7).

Stephen was a man of strong faith. His name means "crown" or "wreath" in Greek. He was appointed to assist the apostles after it became clear that they needed more leaders to help in the administration of the growing church. He served faithfully but was eventually murdered by freedmen: *"And they stoned Stephen as he was calling on God, saying, 'Lord Jesus, receive my spirit.'" Then he knelt down and cried out with a loud voice, "Lord, do not charge them with this sin." And*

141

when he had said this, he fell asleep" (Act 7:59-60) Stephen was a great servant under the apostles. He proved clearly that even a novice can make a positive impact for the Gospel. He eventually became known as a man full of the Holy Ghost, faith, and power. He did great wonders and signs among the people. This man was only a server of tables, yet he was able to witness for the Lord and he made Christ proud of him. He served the apostles and the people. He was not ashamed to be a servant. Part of his service might have been to provide for the poor and "wash the feet" of the apostles, and he was a humble man in whom God magnified Himself.

As a servant in today's world, try to picture yourself as Stephen. Imagine what he had to endure in order to remain faithful. Had any of us been in his place, we would have found it hard to cope. It must be admitted that Stephen was tougher than most of us. No wonder the Holy Spirit filled him to overflowing.

Most in our generation wish to aim high in the ministry, but are not willing to pay the price. There is no shortcut; the way to the top is from the bottom of the ladder. Driven, ambitious people are everywhere, but they submit to no spiritual authority. There is not a pastor or minister, who can fully identify them for their faithfulness.

Clearly, the scripture shows that Stephen became a powerful man full of faith. There was a bold fierceness about his anointing, and this gave the enemy camp a reason to want to attack him. The anointing upon Stephen caused them many a sleepless night. This would not have happened if he had not submitted himself to the mentorship of the apostles.

"And Stephen, full of faith and power, did great wonders and signs among the people. Then there arose some from what is called the Synagogue of the Freedmen (Cyrenians, Alexandrians, and those from Cilicia and Asia), disputing with Stephen. And they were not able to resist the wisdom and the Spirit by which he spoke. Then they secretly induced men to say, 'We have heard him speak blasphemous words against Moses and God.' And they stirred up the people, the elders, and the scribes; and they came upon him, seized him, and brought him to the council. They also set up false witnesses who said, 'This man does not cease to speak blasphemous words against this holy place and the law; for we have heard him say that this Jesus of Nazareth will destroy this place and change the customs which Moses delivered to us.' And all who sat in the council, looking steadfastly at him, saw his face as the face of an angel" (Acts 6:8-15).

Today, there are more people than ever dying because of their faith in Christ. Persecution against Christians is an ongoing practice in various parts of the world. Few of these heroes are remembered and revered for their bravery.

"But he, being full of the Holy Spirit, gazed into heaven and saw the glory of God, and Jesus standing at the right hand of God, and said, 'Look! I see the heavens opened and the Son of Man standing at the right hand of God!' Then they cried out with a loud voice, stopped their ears, and ran at him with one accord; and they cast him out of the city and stoned him. And the witnesses laid down their clothes at the feet of a young man named Saul. And they stoned Stephen as he was calling on God and saying, 'Lord Jesus, receive my spirit.' Then he knelt down and cried out with a loud voice, 'Lord, lay not this sin to

their charge.' And when he had said this, he fell asleep" (Acts 7:55-60).

Stephen's martyrdom is recorded in Acts 7:60. He was stoned to death, but, even as he died, he prayed for the forgiveness of his persecutors. In addition, even as the rocks battered him, the Lord opened his eyes, and he was able to see the glory that awaited him.

He died in service to God, yet Stephen's ministry still lives on. We who read the Bible know about Stephen and often meditate on his testimony. Clearly, he is a good example of a servant who was used by Holy Ghost because he yielded himself.

As a servant, it is important that your dedication and service be to the Lord and without compromise. Also, bear in mind that God is looking for those who will remain faithful to him. This only comes by grace, and God can provide the ability to keep our commitment and to stay on the right track.

Stephen's death brought revival in the land. Again, realize that his original task was to serve tables, yet God used him to spark revival in his region. Some people complain that they have a calling yet have not been given a chance to preach in their church or place of gathering. If you genuinely feel that you have a calling, stop bragging about it, and do something! You could be useful in the vineyard in many areas. In the church there is ushering, cleaning the church, being a Sunday school teacher, singing in the choir, joining the worship team, playing instruments, and evangelizing, just to name a few.

There are also many things one can do, outside the church to further the work of the Lord: one can visit the sick, the elderly, or patients in a hospital. Visiting prisoners, or spending time with the disadvantaged or the despised. Unfortunately, most seem to want to receive compensation for these services.

"Now those who were scattered after the persecution that arose over Stephen traveled as far as Phoenicia, Cyprus, and Antioch, preaching the word to no one but the Jews only. But some of them were men from Cyprus and Cyrene, who, when they had come to Antioch, spoke to the Hellenists, preaching the Lord Jesus. And the hand of the Lord was with them, and a great number believed and turned to the Lord" (Acts 11:19-21).

Many received revelation after Stephen's persecution, and more souls came to Christ just because *one* faithful servant loved Christ more than his own life.

Daniel 9:3 – Then I set my face toward the Lord God to make request by prayer and supplication, with fasting, sackcloth, and ashes

Chapter Fourteen

Find a Partner with a Similar Vision
"I and My House Shall Serve the Lord"

"After these things Paul departed from Athens and went to Corinth. And he found a certain Jew named Aquila, born in Pontus, who had recently come from Italy with his wife Priscilla (because Claudius had commanded all the Jews to depart from Rome); and he came to them. So, because he was of the same trade, he stayed with them and worked, for by occupation they were tentmakers. And he reasoned in the synagogue every Sabbath, and persuaded both Jews and Greeks. When Silas and Timothy had come from Macedonia, Paul was compelled by the Spirit, and testified to the Jews that Jesus is the Christ. But when they opposed him and blasphemed, he shook his garments and said to them, 'Your blood be upon your own heads; I am clean. From now on I will go to the Gentiles'" (Acts 18:1-6).

Priscilla means "ancient, old-fashioned simplicity." "Priscilla" is the diminutive form of "Prisca", as "Johnny" is the diminutive form of "John". Literarily, it means "little Prisca" Diminutives are more common in foreign languages (Latin, Spanish, Russian, Greek) than in English. They can denote affection, or distinguish a younger person from an older, especially a relative with the same name. It can therefore be concluded that Prisca and Priscilla are the same person. Aquila, Priscilla's husband's name, means "eagle" – emblem of the Roman army. According to studies, both names are of Roman origin.

147

It is believed that Priscilla belonged to a distinguished Roman family. Both Priscilla and Aquila were honored and much loved by the apostle Paul and became effective as a couple in serving him in the ministry. Priscilla's name was mentioned with that of her husband in most scriptures, and this would imply that they were partners in the Lord.

Upon his arrival to Corinth, the apostle Paul met Priscilla (or Prisca) and her husband Aquila, who were tentmakers by profession. The apostle joined them in the profession and soon became fond of them. He frequently mentioned their names in his letters. While on a trip with Paul, Priscilla and Aquila met a man named Apollos who had the knowledge of God, but knew only what John the Baptist preached. He was not aware that Christ had already come:

"Now a certain Jew named Apollos, born at Alexandria, an eloquent man and mighty in the Scriptures, came to Ephesus. This man had been instructed in the way of the Lord; and being fervent in spirit, he spoke and taught accurately the things of the Lord, though he knew only the baptism of John. So he began to speak boldly in the synagogue. When Aquila and Priscilla heard him, they took him aside and explained to him the way of God more accurately" (Acts 18:24-26).

It is likely that Apollos heard the message preached by John the Baptist and was convicted that all must repent and return to God. In those days, people were expecting the coming of the Messiah and began to wonder whether John was the Messiah.

"Now as the people were in expectation, and all reasoned in their hearts about John, whether he was the Christ or not, John answered, saying to

148

all, "I indeed baptize you with water; but One mightier than I is coming, whose sandal strap I am not worthy to loose. He will baptize you with the Holy Spirit and fire." (Luke 3:15,16).

Priscilla and Aquila seized upon every opportunity to present the Gospel and applied wisdom whenever needed. They came across Apollos preaching the Word of God. He was eloquent and zealous to let people know the need for repentance. However, he had heard only a portion of the Gospel; he was unaware that the Christ whom John and the Prophets spoke of had already come.

Priscilla and Aquila were already seasoned believers. When they heard Apollos preaching, they knew that they had to update him because the good news by John had become much better news through Christ. They used wisdom when they spoke to him. They did not criticize Apollos publicly, but instead took him aside privately and explained the Gospel more fully to him. It is believed Apollos was encouraged and as a result became much more effective in his preaching.

This is amazing. We frequently hear Christian leaders competing and seeking to outshine one another. Our ministries cannot be effective when everyone thinks of themselves more knowledgeable and talented than others. United we stand, divided we fall. Sometimes, it seems as if these preachers actually look for others to make a mistake just so they can pounce on them and gain an advantage. The good message becomes overshadowed by vain competition and negative comments made by one preacher against another's ministry. Who knows how many non-believers are there who have been convicted to believe in Christ, but are turned off as they see us striving with one another. We need to clean up our act. *Matthew 12:25 states, "But Jesus knew their thoughts, and said to them: 'Every Kingdom divided against itself is brought to desolation, and every city or house divided against itself will not stand.'"* We need unity among believers so that we change the world for Christ.

Priscilla and Aquila did an excellent job of sharing Christ's message with Apollos without embarrassing him. They ministered to this man, who was so fervent in spirit and hungry to learn.

We must witness with love and must humbly take every opportunity whenever it comes. The harvest is plentiful, but the laborers are few. There are many laborers, whose witness lacks effectiveness because they lack vital biblical knowledge.

Moreover, there are members of other faiths who are so deceived that they imagine being a suicide bomber is an effective way to express their faith and convince the world to turn to Allah. Oh, that someone full of the Spirit could gain their trust, show them Christ's love, and teach them the actual truth.

Priscilla and Aquila were deeply involved in the work of God. Some speculate that since the apostle Paul did not sign the epistle to the Hebrews, they might have been involved in writing it under the Apostle Paul's influence. Priscilla was a brave person with strong faith, working as a teammate with Aquila, and together they passionately did ministry. They risked much and trod on new and risky ground as they planted churches with Paul. They were one in the Lord and shared the Spirit's supernatural experience and zeal.

Although Priscilla seemed to possess more zeal than Aquila, there was no indication of strife between them. Their relationship was fascinating, an extraordinary union of two servants of the Lord. They were inseparable soul mates, a selfless couple compatible in their calling and with each other. This was a divine union.

In the service of our Lord, a cooperative husband or wife helps ease the burden. Sometimes a need may arise where one might have to share more of the burden than the other did, and on those occasions, they must understand each other.

Priscilla and Aquila welcomed the apostle Paul to their home. They started a home fellowship, which grew into a church. In fact, they seem to have allowed their home to be used as headquarters for the church. They offered their house to Paul and made him comfortable whenever he boarded with them. Priscilla and Aquila went through storms with Paul, and it would not have been possible for them to stick by Paul had they not agreed as a couple:

"Greet Priscilla and Aquila, my fellow workers in Christ Jesus, who risked their own necks for my life, to whom not only I give thanks, but also all the churches of the Gentiles. Likewise greet the church that is in their house. Greet my beloved Epaenetus, who is the first fruits of Achaia to Christ" (Romans 16:3-5).

Apostle Paul's ministry was full of controversy. On one occasion, they lowered him down through a window so he could escape from a town. He appeared to cause major havoc in the enemy's camp every time he is in a city:

"The God and Father of our Lord Jesus Christ, who is blessed forever, knows that I am not lying. In Damascus the governor, under Aretas the King, was guarding the city of the Damascenes with a garrison, desiring to arrest me; but I was let down in a basket through a window in the wall, and escaped from his hands" (2 Corinthians 11:31-33).

Indeed, serving with him meant laying one's neck on the line, yet this couple overlooked the dangers for the sake of the Gospel. Paul always carried their memory with him wherever he went. On various occasions Paul mentioned their names in his letters and recognized their service to the work of God:

"The churches of Asia greet you. Aquila and Priscilla greet you heartily in the Lord, with the church that is in their house. All the brethren greet you. Greet one another with a holy kiss. The salutation with my own hand--Paul's. If anyone does not love the Lord Jesus Christ, let him be accursed. O Lord, come! The grace of our Lord Jesus Christ be with you. My love be with you all in Christ Jesus. Amen" (1 Corinthians 16: 19-24; Also, see 2 Timothy 4:19).

You seldom hear mentors extend their appreciation to those serving them. Priscilla and Aquila were not just servants; they were "armor bearers." Paul sailed with them to Syria.. *(Then he took leave of the brethren and sailed for Syria, and*

152

Priscilla and Aquila were with him. He had his hair cut off at Cenchrea, for he had taken a vow" Acts 18:18).

This couple has shown us that it is possible for a husband and wife to serve together in the work of the Lord and enjoy it. It is speculated that they were saints eventually killed because of the Gospel. Whether they died naturally or were murdered, their life is worth celebrating for the good course they took for the Gospel. They became like the ancient eagle, soaring higher and higher, extending the Gospel to the nations of the world.

Proverbs 7:15 – So I came out to meet you, Diligently to seek your face, And I have found you.

Chapter Fifteen

A Faithful Servant
Know Your Place

Timothy's name is of Greek origin and means "God's honor." Timothy was an energetic, well-trained, young Christian and a companion of the apostle, Paul, who wrote to him, "Let no man look down on your youth." It is said that Timothy was martyred after denouncing worshippers of the Greek moon goddess, Diana.

The apostle Paul spoke well of Timothy, and so did the brethren at Lystra and Iconium. Timothy had a good name and good reputation *("A good name is more to be desired than great riches, Loving favor rather than silver and gold" (Proverbs 22:1).*

Paul was encouraged by the people's testimony about Timothy. It inspired him to keep Timothy active in the ministry. He adopted him as his spiritual son. The Word tells us that these two servants of the Lord blessed churches. It is important that the servant be able to submit to his master so an impartation can take place. This is needed so the master can do what is necessary, both spiritually and physically, to prepare the servant for the godly assignment.

"Then he came to Derbe and Lystra. And behold, a certain disciple was there, named Timothy, the son of a certain Jewish woman

who believed, but his father was Greek. He was well spoken of by the brethren who were at Lystra and Iconium. Paul wanted to have him go on with him. And he took him and circumcised him because of the Jews who were in that region, for they all knew that his father was Greek. And as they went through the cities, they delivered to them the decrees to keep, which were determined by the apostles and elders at Jerusalem. So the churches were strengthened in the faith, and increased in number daily." (Act 16: 1-5)

Paul referred to Timothy as his fellow worker *(Romans 16:21)*, as a beloved and faithful son in the Lord *(see 1 Corinthians 4:17)*, and as a brother. And in one of his letters to the Philippians, Paul referred to Timothy and himself as bondservants of Jesus Christ *(Philippians 1:1)*.

Paul made sure that Timothy grew up in the calling, and he came to value Timothy's input, always speaking very highly of him. He did everything possible to help Timothy rise in ministry. As an elder in spiritual matters, Paul was the best person to guide Timothy.

We can only hope that God will rise up many "Paul's" in our generation. Today there are many wasted talents wandering here and there, lacking insight and direction. Those we wish we could look up to are often only interested in building their own kingdoms, if one tries to succeed under them; they end up frustrating the person's efforts.

Paul covered Timothy's back as any great friend would---to the point of telling people to treat Timothy well. He ordered them to support Timothy in every possible way wherever he was on a mission. Paul knew a servant is worthy of respect, and he did not feel threatened by projecting Timothy as a co-leader in the church.

Some servants have delayed in maturing in the call of God because of oppression from their masters. Such oppressors will be held accountable to the Master for their ill motives toward those whom God has placed under them.

"Now if Timothy comes, see that he may be with you without fear; for he does the work of the Lord, as I also do. Therefore, let no one despise him. But send him on his journey in peace, that he may come to me; for I am waiting for him with the brethren" (1 Corinthians 16: 10-11).

Timothy was trained by Paul to preach *(see 2 Corinthians 1: 19)* and to build up the churches. Humility and sincerity are desirable qualities for one to possess. This is worthy in serving the Lord and making the job easier for his or her master. A person filled with the Holy Spirit would make a good mediator between the master and the people. A servant should be capable of giving an honest report without bias, not withholding anything that could jeopardize the ministry. Wisdom becomes handy to avoid unnecessary confrontation.

"But now that Timothy has come to us from you, and brought us good news of your faith and love, and that you always have good remembrance of us, greatly desiring to see us, as we also to see you" (1 Thessalonians 3:6).

Timothy must have become a very good communicator and most likely possessed good interpersonal skills. He accurately relayed Paul's message wherever he was sent and brought feedback to the apostle. *(Philippians 2:19, and 1 Thessalonians 3:2)*. He could not have done this if he was not well trained by Paul.

1 Thessalonians 3:2 - and sent Timothy, our brother and minister of God, and our fellow laborer in the gospel of Christ, to establish you and encourage you concerning your faith,

Timothy was a man who was well groomed, and possessed a good character and a positive attitude. He was not a mischievous person looking for ways to take over Paul's job. When people saw Timothy it was as though they had seen Paul.

Is this possible in our day? We are living in a rebellious generation and many have departed from the ways of God. As a universal Church, we lack compassion, yet we claim to be used by God. We can see this lack of submission in both masters and servants. How can a servant be submissive if all they see is arrogance in those under whom they serve?

We need to pray for God's intervention so we can, by God's grace, advance the work that God has called us to do. Prayer can overturn negative situations. Timothy must have been a prayerful person, for there is no way he could have achieved all that he did without being in direct communication with heaven. Prayer is the *key;* it enables the servant to stand in the gap against the schemes of the enemy: *"This charge I commit to you, son Timothy, according to the prophecies previously made concerning you, that by them you may wage the good warfare" (1 Timothy 1:18).*

Paul coached Timothy to wage war with the promises and prophecies that were given to him. Satan is aware that one's destiny is planned before birth, but he does not make it easy for the person to attain their destiny. Of course, Christ already won these battles for us and prayer helps to facilitate God's purpose in our lives.

It is our responsibility to gain knowledge and understanding of who we are in Christ. We need to know what is required to achieve our victory through Christ. Sound biblical knowledge keeps our minds in perfect peace. The Lord said, *"Peace I leave with you, My peace I give to you; not as the world gives do I give to you. Let not your heart be troubled, neither let it be afraid." (John 14:27).*

Distraction can come in any form, be it sickness, other people, or a government system. Studying the Word, praying, and fasting will equip us throughout our journey to the "Promised Land."

Paul was a master of spiritual warfare. In his lifetime he fought many fierce battles and managed to fulfill the purpose of God concerning his ministry. Through Christ, there was no battle too intimidating for Paul, and he overcame them all.

As a servant of God, some battles may manifest themselves through the discouragement of others. They tell you that you are wasting your time and that you will never amount to anything. These people, whether they mean it or not, are saying all these evil things so you will give up on your dreams. However, as long as you keep yourself pure, God will order your footsteps. Despite all that faces you, let each trying experience toughen you and make you stronger.

Others might have discouraged Timothy. His master prayed for him that he be strengthened. Timothy was made aware of the battles so he would war against them. Paul also challenged him not to allow others to despise his youthfulness.

"O Timothy! Guard what was committed to your trust, avoiding the profane and idle babblings and contradictions of what is falsely called knowledge-- by professing it some have strayed concerning the faith. Grace be with you. Amen" (1 Timothy 6:20-21).

Timothy went through much as a servant of God and it appears that he may even have faced imprisonment for a time. *"Know that our brother Timothy has been set free, with whom I shall see you if he comes shortly" (Hebrews 13:23).*

He paid the ultimate price all the way; there was no holding back as far as he was concerned. A servant should always bear in mind that serving Christ is an "all the way" journey. After all, Christ is the great Master, suffered the utmost for our sake.

"Let as many bondservants as are under the yoke count their own masters worthy of all honor, so that the name of God and His doctrine may not be blasphemed. And those who have believing masters, let them not despise them because they are brethren, but rather serve

them because those who are benefited are believers and beloved. Teach and exhort these things. If anyone teaches otherwise and does not consent to wholesome words, even the words of our Lord Jesus Christ, and to the doctrine which accords with godliness, he is proud, knowing nothing, but is obsessed with disputes and arguments over words, from which come envy, strife, reviling, evil suspicions, useless wrangling of men of corrupt minds and destitute of the truth, who suppose that godliness is a means of gain. From such withdraw yourself" (1 Timothy 6:1-5).

Paul was a great mentor to Timothy. He taught him to respect those who were ruling over him and to be submissive as well. It is important for us who want to be used by God to follow Timothy's example about our spiritual leaders. Their prayers and blessings provide a spiritual covering that we need in our assignments. It is always important to be accountable to others, rather than keeping our affairs secret. For example, we might want to attend a meeting or perhaps have been invited to minister. It is good to let our mentor know of opportunities, as well as obstacles, successes, and questions. Accountability can spare us from unnecessary battles. Scripture instructs us: *"Obey those who rule over you, and be submissive, for they watch out for your souls, as those who must give account. Let them do so with joy and not with grief, for that would be unprofitable for you"* (Hebrews 13:17).

Paul was always proud of Timothy, and was joyful whenever he thought of him *(2 Timothy 1:1-14)*. Timothy, being a young man could sometimes not hold back his tears, probably having seen the suffering Paul had to go through for the Gospel. Paul advised Timothy to exercise the gift of God which Timothy received by the laying on of Paul's hands. Paul made Timothy aware that Christ calls us to a

161

holy calling, not according to our works, but according to His own purpose and grace, which was given to us in Christ Jesus. Many times, he kept reminding Timothy to guard the calling that was given to him. He urged Timothy to be bold and not to be ashamed of the testimony of our Lord Jesus Christ. Paul also monitored Timothy's conduct and corrected him with wisdom whenever necessary. Timothy turned out to be one of the best ministers under Paul. He was a blessed man to have Paul as his mentor.

It is exceptional in these last days to find mentors, like Paul, who are ready to share wisdom gleaned through decades of experience. Through their nurture, servants can reach their full potential in the things of God. Paul did not care at all about his own fame, finances, or number of followers. He realized that the kingdoms of this world will not last, but the Kingdom of our God will last forever, and he wanted to mobilize as many as possible to help him reach the world.

Some Christian leaders actually feel more intimidated when servants begin to operate in the gifts of the Holy Spirit. They begin to look for ways to stop them or at least slow them down. They worry that a popular individual on the ministerial staff may steal the congregation's loyalty or affection. They feel too intimidated to set the staff free to use their gifts to ultimate advantage in the body.

The mentor needs to understand when one's time has come to be used of God more independently. Eventually, Timothy did not need as much coaching or supervision from Paul. However, their close friendship continued to deepen.

Fellowship between a master and a servant can continue even after the servant has ventured into his or her own ministry. The master can provide spiritual cover if the two are still on good terms with one another.

Even though Timothy began to travel to churches, he still submitted himself to Paul's authority. He was always available when Paul needed him. As a servant, you can continue to learn new things from your master, even while you are out on your own. Your destiny and relationship with your mentor depends on whether he or she loves the Lord deeply enough to care for willing novices who need a shepherd.

Conversely, while the Holy Spirit's presence was a comfort to Paul, Timothy was greatly used by God as an encouragement to Paul during some of his darkest hours. Paul wrote to Timothy: *"This you know, that all those in Asia have turned away from me, among whom are Phygellus and Hermogenes" (2 Timothy 1:15).*

We need to value correction from our mentors, realizing that, though it may be painful, it is worthwhile. A good mentor will be attentive to the well being of his or her protégés.

Paul was confident that Timothy could carry on the work of the ministry in his absence.

"Only let your conduct be worthy of the gospel of Christ, so that whether I come and see you or am absent, I may hear of your affairs,

that you stand fast in one spirit, with one mind striving together for the faith of the gospel." (Philippians 1:27)

He trained Timothy in practical experience as well as spiritual. He had no reason to doubt that Timothy would represent Christ well because Timothy proved he could do any assignment that was given to him.

"But I trust in the Lord Jesus to send Timothy to you shortly, that I also may be encouraged when I know your state. For I have no one like-minded, who will sincerely care for your state. For all seek their own, not the things which are of Christ Jesus. But you know his proven character, that as a son with his father he served with me in the gospel. Therefore I hope to send him at once, as soon as I see how it goes with me. But I trust in the Lord that I myself shall also come shortly" (Philippians 2:19-24).

There were consequences for those who disobeyed Paul, for they were actually rebelling against Christ. *"This charge I commit to you, son Timothy, according to the prophecies previously made concerning you, that by them you may wage the good warfare, having faith and a good conscience, which some having rejected, concerning the faith have suffered shipwreck, of whom are Hymeneals and Alexander, whom I delivered to Satan that they may learn not to blaspheme"* (1 Timothy 1: 18-20).

Disobedience to our mentor can result in grave consequences. Never speak against your mentor, even if he or she is wrong. Leave it to God. In all the years I have served my mentor, Dr. Manton, I have never heard him speak against any man or woman of God, and he always speaks most highly of those who formerly mentored him.

"For the Lord will judge His people, And He will have compassion on His servants" (Psalms 135:14).

Paul noted that some of the members who were serving with Timothy were seeking their own way instead of doing the things which are of Christ Jesus. These immature believers thought they had 'matured', and were not willing to submit to anyone. Wide is the road of the arrogant; narrow is the path of the meek.

Moving from a servant to a powerful minister, Timothy began to tackle major tasks as seen in the scripture below. He would not have been able to differentiate and clarify doctrines had he not received sound teaching from Paul.

"As I urged you when I went into Macedonia--remain in Ephesus that you may charge some that they teach no other doctrine, nor give heed to fables and endless genealogies, which cause disputes rather than godly edification which is in faith. Now the purpose of the commandment is love from a pure heart, from a good conscience, and from sincere faith, from which some, having strayed, have turned aside to idle talk" (1 Timothy 1:3-6).

Having submitted himself to Paul's leadership, Timothy became a powerful man of God just like his mentor. May God give us a teachable spirit like Timothy so that we can excel in our calling to the glory of God.

Jeremiah 33:2-3 — "Thus says the Lord who made it, the Lord who formed it to establish it (the Lord is His name); 'Call to Me, and I will answer you, and show you great and mighty things, which you do not know.'

Chapter Sixteen

Jesus: The Greatest Servant-Leader
Serve with Your Whole Heart

So it was, as the multitude pressed about Him to hear the word of God, that He stood by the Lake of Gennesaret, and saw two boats standing by the lake; but the fishermen had gone from them and were washing their nets. Then He got into one of the boats, which was Simon's, and asked him to put out a little from the land. And He sat down and taught the multitudes from the boat. When He had stopped speaking, He said to Simon, "Launch out into the deep and let down your nets for a catch." But Simon answered and said to Him, "Master, we have toiled all night and caught nothing; nevertheless at Your word I will let down the net." And when they had done this, they caught a great number of fish, and their net was breaking. So they signaled to their partners in the other boat to come and help them. And they came and filled both the boats, so that they began to sink. When Simon Peter saw it, he fell down at Jesus' knees, saying, "Depart from me, for I am a sinful man, O Lord!" (Luke 5:1-8)

Meeting the Lord turned Peter from an ordinary fisherman into a fisher of men as the Lord intended. This was the beginning of Peter's transformation. The Lord stressed that whoever wants to be with Him must separate themselves from earthly pleasures and not cling to earthly possessions *(See Luke 14:26-33)*. The Lord wanted commitment from His disciples so they would remain focused on assignments with no interference.

167

Jesus even taught the importance of being law-abiding citizens. This was obvious in Capernaum when those who received the temple tax wanted to know whether Christ paid taxes. The Lord directed Peter to go fish, find a coin in a fish's mouth and pay them on His behalf and Peter's *(See Matthew 17: 24-27)*.

Unlike most people today who do not want to be associated with serving, or be called servants, the Lord's emphasis was that whoever wants to be great must become the least. He portrayed this by washing His disciples' feet and asking them to serve menially in many ways.

"In the beginning was the Word and the Word was with God, and the Word was God. He was in the beginning with God. All things were made through Him, and without Him nothing was made that was made. In Him was life, and the life was the light of men" John 1:1-4).

The prophets spoke of the coming of Messiah who will bring salvation to humankind. Isaiah saw the beautiful feet of the Lord. *"How beautiful upon the mountains are the feet of him who brings good news, who proclaims peace, who brings glad tidings of good things, who proclaims salvation, who says to Zion, "Your God reigns!" (Isaiah 52:7).*

Jeremiah prophesied that the Lord would come to execute judgment and righteousness in the earth. *"Behold, the days are coming,' says the Lord, 'that I will perform that good thing which I have promised to the house of Israel and to the house of Judah: 'In those days and at that time I will cause to grow up to David A*

Branch of righteousness; He shall execute judgment and righteousness in the earth" (Jeremiah 33:14-15).

There were many expectations of His coming. When a Samaritan woman met the Lord, she said, *"I know that Messiah is coming" (who is called Christ). "When He comes, He will tell us all things." Jesus said to her, "I who speak to you am He" (John 4:25-26).*

John the Baptist witnessed that he saw the Spirit descending from heaven like a dove, and the Holy Spirit remained upon the Lord. Luke wrote that a voice came from heaven which said, *"You are My beloved Son; in You I am well pleased" (John 1:32, Luke 3:22).* After His baptism, the Holy Spirit led the Lord to the wilderness where he was tempted and was found blameless *(Mark 1:12-14).*

After Christ's victory in the wilderness, the people in Galilee began to accept him. He returned in the power of the Spirit into Galilee, and word of Him spread through all the surrounding regions. He taught in their synagogues, being glorified by all. In Nazareth, where He had been brought up, and according to the custom of that day, He went into the synagogue on the Sabbath day, and stood up to read from the book of Isaiah. The Bible says people were amazed at the wisdom with which Christ was speaking.

Our Master had been to the wilderness, and He came out victorious so that by following His example, we too can conquer wilderness battles. Satan tempted Him with offers in an attempt to convince Him to give up the cross, but the Lord based His defence on the scripture.

Many with a calling have given up halfway to their destination because of temptations. Spiritual victory does not come easily, but only through obedience to Christ. We are required to obey God, and this goes hand-in-hand with denying oneself. Temptations to win victories which will only please the Evil One come with loose freebees without restriction. It is easy to be fooled by Satan's counterfeits. But giving in to this travesty will only result in long-term regret and the perishing of one's vision. Jesus triumphed over Satan in the wilderness temptations; then He went on to launch His public ministry. At the synagogue he read the scripture below.

"The Spirit of the Lord is upon Me, because He has anointed Me to preach the gospel to the poor; he has sent Me to heal the broken hearted, to proclaim liberty to the captives and recovery of sight to the blind, to set at liberty those who are oppressed" (Luke 4:18).

After reading the above scripture, the Lord closed the book, and He gave it back to the minister and sat down. The eyes of all them that were in the synagogue were fastened on him. The Lord sensed the people's thoughts were negative toward him. He told them that there were many widows in the days of Elijah when the heavens were shut up for three years and six months, and there was a great famine throughout all the land; but Elijah was sent to none of them except to Zarephath, to a widow who lived in the region of Sidon. The Lord said there were many lepers in Israel during the time of Elisha the prophet, and none of them was cleansed except Naaman the Syrian (Luke 4:25-27).

We must seek God and make ourselves available for His grace in our lives as Shunammite woman did. Then God will take us under His wing, train us, and begin giving us assignments. These could be revealed either through a mentor, a prophetic word, vision, dream, or peace within one's soul. At your place of assignment, you will receive grace and provision to move forward with what God has assigned you in that place and among those people.

Disciples were trained by Christ to be apostles after the Lord's ascension; therefore, there was need for them to understand how important it was to serve. Christ led by example as an obedient servant to God. He was aware of the pain that He would go through as a sacrificial lamb for our reunion with God. Despite that, He remained obedient to God. He could have refused, but, instead, submitted to the will of His Father *(Matthew 26:42)*.

The Lord taught His disciples how to pray intensely. The scriptures reveal that the Lord himself prayed until His sweat became like great drops of blood falling to the ground. The Bible says the Lord was in agony. Following His example, we should yield more to God in prayer and ask fervently for His will in our lives. Jesus Christ, our Master and Lord showed us there is a great need to wage war through prayer. Our prayer life must improve, even though the Spirit of the Lord is interceding for us *(Luke 22:44; Romans 8:26)*.

Although at the time of crucifixion Peter denied three times that he knew the Lord, he later came to his senses. From the beginning of his encounter with the Lord, Peter acknowledged that he was a sinful man. He desired to do the will of God although he was also battling with his inner self, which let him down on a few occasions, yet, this was not a surprise because we see earlier the Lord saying to him that Satan had planned to sift Peter as a wheat but He had prayed for him. Amazingly, Peter in his human nature could not have foreseen this coming. He assured the Lord that he would stick by him even to death. Luke 22:31-34 And *the Lord said, "Simon, Simon! Indeed, Satan has asked for you, that he may sift you as wheat. But I have prayed for you, that your faith should not fail; and when you have returned to Me, strengthen your brethren." But he said to Him, "Lord, I am ready to go with You, both to prison and to death." Then He said, "I tell you, Peter, the rooster shall not crow this day before you will deny three times that you know Me."*

Apostle Peter denied three times that he knew the Lord (Matthew 26:74 -75). Yet, what the Lord saw concerning Peter, happened. This was Peter's wilderness moment. Many like Peter, have desired to follow the Lord in spite of trials and temptation. However, victory can be achieved if one is at the right place. Doing so will impart knowledge to the individual concern that if the Lord prayed for Peter then He is also doing the same for us today. There is no struggle that we go through that is unknown to the Lord. However, we have a responsibility to play a role by understanding our authority in the Word. Studying Apostles Peter and Paul, we see two great men who had strong desire to do the will of God. They clearly portrayed that it is possible for one to triumph over fleshly desire and posses a destiny purposed by God. Apostle Paul mentioned in one of his letters that the things, which happened to him, have turned out for the furtherance of the gospel. In this regard, whatever you are going through at this moment could be your pathway to the destiny that God has for you – Philippians 1:12-13

One could only imagine the amount of guilty Peter had to deal with the information that Christ was the Messiah. *Matthew 16:16 Simon Peter answered and said, "You are the Christ, the Son of the living God."* The Spirit of God revealed to him who Jesus was as seen in the scriptures. No wonder he was the devil's target. The enemy knew that Peter was destined to be the rock, which Christ later said upon him, He would build His Church. However, at his testing time Apostle Peter learnt a lot which became useful in empowering believers. This is seen in his epistles whereby he is cautioning us to be careful. In his epistles he covered subjects on life style of a believer and ability to distinguish between doctrines. He emphasized on holiness and the need to gird the loins of our mind with understanding that the Word of God lives and abide forever. In the wilderness is where we really get revelation of who God is and who we are in Him if we choose to believe. By saying this, we have seen God in His majestic ways-providing manner for the Israelites in the wilderness. Although one could dismiss this as just food, it is beyond anyone's comprehension at what level God would come through when we need Him at our lowest point in life. At this point is when our faith increases and we get closer to Him if we stop complaining.

When Christ arose from the dead He called the twelve disciples to Himself and gave them power over unclean spirits---power to cast out demons and to heal all kinds of sicknesses and diseases. Their impartation from the Lord was not automatic. He had to pray for the disciples. They had been obedient and had served Him, yet Christ had to pass on the power to them *(See Matthew 10:1).*

Masters should pray for their servants to have impartation so they can accomplish their appointed ministry at the appointed time. There may be someone reading this that has not had a good send-off because of some misunderstanding with his or her mentor. You wonder what will happen to you because of that. There are cases in which only God can intervene. It is not what man wants, but what is best and fair in the eyes of God that counts in our ministries. If anyone tries to hinder the vision that He has imparted to us, God will come to our defense so long as we are right with Him.

If, despite all efforts, one has served well and left a ministry because a matter could not be resolved due to motives beyond one's control, God will give grace and that impartation of Himself. In this I mean if you have left quietly without evil motives, the Lord will defend you. Thus, in every case it is important as a servant to do your best to make sure that your actions are in line with the Word of God.

"For the Kingdom of heaven is like a man traveling to a far country, who called his own servants and delivered his goods to them. Moreover, to one he gave five talents, to another two, and to another one, to each according to his own ability; and immediately he went on a journey. Then he who had received the five talents went and traded with them, and made another five talents. And likewise he who had received

174

two gained two more also. But he who had received one went and dug in the ground, and hid his lord's money.

After a long time the lord of those servants came and settled accounts with them. So he who had received five talents came and brought five other talents, saying, 'Lord, you delivered to me five talents; look, I have gained five more talents besides them.' His lord said to him, 'Well done, good and faithful servant; you were faithful over a few things, I will make you ruler over many things. Enter into the joy of your lord.' He also who had received two talents came and said, 'Lord, you delivered to me two talents; look, I have gained two more talents besides them.' His lord said to him, 'Well done, good and faithful servant; you have been faithful over a few things, I will make you ruler over many things. Enter into the joy of your lord.'

Then he who had received the one talent came and said, 'Lord, I knew you to be a hard man, reaping where you have not sown, and gathering where you have not scattered seed. And I was afraid, and went and hid your talent in the ground. Look, there you have what is yours.' But his lord answered and said to him, 'You wicked and lazy servant, you knew that I reap where I have not sown, and gather where I have not scattered seed. So you ought to have deposited my money with the bankers, and at my coming I would have received back my own with interest." (Matthew 25: 14-27).

Therefore take the talent from him, and give it to him who has ten talents. For to everyone who has, more will be given, and he will have abundance; but from him who does not have, even what he has will be taken away. And cast the unprofitable servant into the outer darkness. There will be weeping and gnashing of teeth.' "When the Son of Man comes in His glory, and all the holy angels with Him, then He will sit on the throne of His glory. All the nations will be gathered before Him, and He will separate them one from another, as a shepherd divides his sheep from the goats. (Matthew 25: 28 -32).

The parable of the ten talents applied to those in Christ's day, and consequently, to us too. Every one of us can do something to enable the Gospel reach places we never heard of or knew of. The Lord expects us to use the gifts that He has given each one of us to enhance the Kingdom of God. At His return, He will inquire what each of us has done with them. He wants us, as disciples, to be aware that we must put to use the knowledge that is given to us.

Paul wrote about the Kingdom of God in *Romans 14:17: "For the Kingdom of God is not eating and drinking, but righteousness and peace and joy in the Holy Ghost."*

God the Father allowed Jesus thirty years on earth before He began His ministry. Moreover, Jesus devoted three years with His disciples to train them to become fishers of men. Being with the Lord was wonderful; however, the disciples did not understand fully their predicament.

Sometimes we fail to appreciate what we have until it ends; and that is when reality hits home. The Lord looked after the disciples, paid their taxes, protected them, and prayed for them. They did not have to fast like John's disciples, though the Lord made them aware that a time would come when they would have to put into good use what they had learned from Him, including fasting and praying.

This principle is applicable even for us today. We may be serving under a ministry, and all may seem well. We think that anyone could do it, but then the storms and opposition hit and we gradually begin to learn what it takes to achieve victory in ministry.

The Lord experienced the awful travail of atonement and then spiritual childbirth to make it possible for each soul on earth to be born into His family and come into communion with Almighty God. This is an overwhelming truth. It is simple to accept, but if one takes time to meditate on the crucifixion, only then can one gain a clear picture of how much God loves each of us.

The disciples experienced a full manifestation of the Kingdom work by their obedience to Christ's teachings. After Jesus ascended, He gave them power, challenging them to wait for the Holy Spirit to come upon them. Moreover, it is just as Paul said; Nothing could come between them and God's love: *"Who shall separate us from the love of Christ? Shall tribulation, or distress, or persecution, or famine, or nakedness, or peril, or sword? As it is written: "For Your sake we are killed all day long; we are accounted as sheep for the slaughter." Yet in all these things we are more than conquerors through Him who loved us"* (Romans 8:35-37).

They lived preaching the Gospel, and some died because of it. They did not compromise, but respectfully served their Master as the Master served His Father – Almighty God. We must make certain we are still on the same course the Lord intended for us. Are our gifts being applied in an appropriate manner? Are we in line with the

Word of God? We must decide whether we truly long to be used by God, and if so, this can only be achieved through humble service: *"Let a man so consider us, as servants of Christ and stewards of the mysteries of God. "Moreover it is required in stewards that a man be found faithful"* (1 Corinthians 4: 1-2).

CONCLUSION

It is my prayer that this book will bring understanding to many who desire to serve our Lord Jesus Christ, that those who are going through the fire will receive hope knowing there is nothing impossible with God. Those of you who are going through physical and spiritual hardship will gain strength through experiences shared in this book. Keep holding on to the promises of God. I pray knowledge will be imparted to both masters and servants to know what is expected of each.

"The mystery which has been hidden from ages and from generations, but now has been revealed to His saints. To them God willed to make known what are the riches of the glory of this mystery among the Gentiles: which is Christ in you, the hope of glory." *(Colossians 1:26 - 27).*

I wish for the words of the apostle, Paul, to be my own: *"For to me, to live is Christ, and to die is gain"* *(Philippians 1:21).*

I love you with the love of the Lord. May God enrich and preserve you in Christ Jesus, Amen.

— Priscar Manei

Leviticus 26:13 – I am the Lord your God, who brought you out of the land of Egypt, that you should not be their slaves; I have broken the bands of your yoke and made you walk upright.

ABOUT THE AUTHOR

Priscar Manei is an anointed prophetic evangelist with a great passion to see souls come to Christ. She was raised in a good Christian home and was dedicated to the path of a ministerial call. The Lord has been preparing her for ministry under the mentorship of several great pastors and leaders. She has served a total of seven years in various capacities, including leading intercession in prayer meetings. She has served the ministry of Dr. Thomas Manton IV; Founder / Overseer of Dominion International in the European Branch for several years. Priscar hosted a weekly Gospel Inspiration a globally radio program and an online e- prayer group 'The Watch and Pray.' She is the Author of In The Secret Place - Conversations With God. Priscar4Jesus@gmail.com

John 17:21 – that they all may be one, as You, Father, are in Me and I in You; that they also may be one in Us, that the world may believe that You sent Me

ORDER FORM

To order <u>autographed</u> copies of this book for family or friends, simply fill in the information below:

PayPal.

dozconnections@gmail.com

YES, I would like to order _____ (quantity) <u>autographed</u> copies of Surviving The Wilderness:
On The Way To Your Destiny. . at **7.49 GBP or $12.99 US ea**.
Please add (£5.00) per book for shipping and handling.
Total enclosed: _____

Your Name:_____

Your address: _____

City/Town: _____

State: _____Zip:_____

Phone: (optional)_____
E-mail: _____

Please allow two weeks for delivery

<u>Non-autographed</u> copies are available on-line at: Amazon.com, Barnes & Noble.com, Borders.com, Mardels.com, Target.com and Books-A-Million.com as well as at numerous bookstores.

www.ingramcontent.com/pod-product-compliance
Lightning Source LLC
Chambersburg PA
CBHW060242050426
42448CB00009B/1551